The Publishing Business

From p-books to e-books

Kelvin Smith

academia

An AVA Book

Published by AVA Publishing SA
Rue des Fontenailles 16
Case Postale
1000 Lausanne 6
Switzerland
Tel: +41 786 005 109
Email: enquiries@avabooks.com

Distributed by Thames & Hudson (ex-North America)
181a High Holborn
London WC1V 7QX
United Kingdom
Tel: +44 20 7845 5000
Fax: +44 20 7845 5055
Email: sales@thameshudson.co.uk
www.thamesandhudson.com

Distributed in the USA & Canada by:
Ingram Publisher Services Inc.
1 Ingram Blvd.
La Vergne TN 37086
USA
Tel: +1 866 400 5351
Fax: +1 800 838 1149
Email: customer.service@ingrampublisherservices.com

English Language Support Office
AVA Publishing (UK) Ltd.
Tel: +44 1903 204 455
Email: enquiries@avabooks.com

© AVA Publishing SA 2012

ISBN 978-2-940411-62-7

Library of Congress Cataloging-in-Publication Data
Smith, Kelvin.
The Publishing Business: From p-books to e-books. / Kelvin Smith p. cm.
Includes bibliographical references and index.
ISBN: 9782940411627 (pbk. :alk. paper)
eISBN: 9782940447374
1. Publishers and publishing. 2. Publishers and publishing -- Technological innovations. 3. Electronic publishing.
Z278 .S557 2012

10 9 8 7 6 5 4 3 2 1

Design by Studio8 Design

Production by AVA Book Production Pte. Ltd., Singapore
Tel: +65 6334 8173
Fax: +65 6259 9830
Email: production@avabooks.com.sg

The Publishing Business

From p-books to e-books

Kelvin Smith

creative careers

Ethical: awareness/reflection/debate

ava academia

Contents

Chapter 5: Design and production

Chapter 6: Print and electronic publishing

Chapter 7: Marketing, sales and distribution

Conclusion

Introduction

The purpose of this book is to teach you something about the many elements that make up modern publishing practice. Publishing is one area where the impact of information technology was felt early on, but for some years this was mainly confined to the 'back office' areas of origination and production of texts and illustrations. In recent years, the effects of the digital culture have swept rapidly through the industry all the way from writers to readers. The way in which publications are written, designed, produced, promoted, distributed and read has changed; and the financial models and legal structures that have been central to publishing for many decades have been challenged.

While many of the practical and professional skills required in publishing today will continue to change as further technology is integrated into the publishing mix, anyone entering the publishing business still needs a fundamental core of specialist knowledge. This includes not only professional skills, but also industry awareness, cultural sensibility and an ability to apply a variety of legal principles and sound planning, budgeting and monitoring tools. This book aims to provide this foundation for anyone planning or entering a career in publishing.

From writer to reader

We explore the book publishing process from writer to reader, passing through the essential publishing activities performed in editorial, design, production and marketing departments. By laying out clearly the tasks and responsibilities at each stage of the publishing process, this book provides a sound basis on which to build. Case studies give examples of publishing practice in different parts of the industry, including children's, academic and trade publishing. Charts and tables provide information on aspects of the industry in an international context.

Review exercises help you to evaluate what you have learned. They help to build your knowledge and skills in making decisions on content and form, and give you practice in formulating the plans, schedules and budgets needed during the book publishing process.

With a sound knowledge of these fundamentals, you will be well prepared to learn more about specialist areas of publishing, and to explore your own path into this challenging and rewarding career.

Preparing for change

This is an exciting time to be starting a career in publishing and *The Publishing Business* introduces you to the profession at a hectic time in its development. The effects of the digital revolution are creating major advances in ways that affect everyone in publishing, whether they are writers, agents, editors, designers, marketers, booksellers, journalists, librarians, or researchers. Therefore, you need to be prepared for change. You need flexibility and imagination, willingness and adaptability if you are to prosper in the publishing future. You also need to understand the context in which publishing has developed and from which it must move forward into a future that will continue to be subject to technological, economic, social and political developments.

'This transformation has been shrouded in something like the fog of war, the smoke and dust from the global IT revolution whose outcome no sensible person can predict, and whose influence touches every aspect of the printed word: books, magazines and newspapers.'

Robert McCrum, the Guardian, *January 2010*

The Publishing Business provides you with ways to understand what book publishing is and what it might become. It encourages you to acquire the skills and knowledge that will be vital to you as you continue your life in publishing. The book aims to make sure that you have a sound foundation on which to base your further studies of editorial, production, marketing, distribution or finance, in whichever specialist area of book publishing may beckon as your career develops.

You will never stop learning about publishing. So now is the time to develop the habit of following up all links and references, grasp new technologies and new business models, read the trade press and specialist websites; never lose an opportunity to see what others are thinking, saying, writing and dreaming about publishing.

Throughout the book you should take the opportunity to stop and think about what you are learning, and to get used to the idea that there are sometimes no right or wrong answers. Good publishing often comes down to sound judgement, and you should make this your goal. Learning about publishing is an ongoing activity and you need to keep an open and agile mind to make sense of the changes that are taking place. This may sound challenging, but it will be worth it!

People and publishing: who does what in book publishing?

Publishing is a 'people business', and to understand book publishing you need to know about who does what in the publishing process. Before you start reading Chapter 1, here is a brief introduction to some types of book publishing and some of the jobs that you will come across in the following chapters. However, job titles are not always used in the same way, and it's often better to look at what people do rather than what they are called. Most people start their career in publishing as an assistant in one of the departments discussed in this section.

In smaller companies, some of the roles may be undertaken by one person, and many jobs are outsourced to freelancers (proofreaders, indexers, picture researchers) and other service companies who can more cost-effectively fulfil specialist functions (software design, distribution, and promotion).

Consumer, trade or general publishing

To some extent, the jobs people do depends on the type of publishing they are engaged in. So it's important to understand what these types of publishing are before we start.

Consumer, trade or general publishing
Publishers of what are variously known as consumer, trade or general publishing books produce novels, biographies, cookery books and so on – books that we read for pleasure in our leisure time. These are primarily sold in bookstores (either physical or online), at airports and stations, and at supermarkets. We may also download books like these from online retailers, or direct from a publisher's website.

Many authors of trade, general or consumer books have an agent (or literary agent) who represents their business interests, helps them to develop a career, and negotiates on their behalf with publishers and others who wish to make use of their clients' work. Some agents now also publish e-books (electronic books) for their clients.

Some major international trade publishers are the Penguin Group, and (in the UK) Hachette, Random House, HarperCollins and Pan Macmillan. The biggest trade publishers in the US are Random House (see page 36), HarperCollins, Simon & Schuster, Penguin, and Hachette. These companies represent most of the imprints we are familiar with, apart from a few medium-sized independents such as Faber and Faber, Canongate and Workman Books.

Educational and ELT publishing
Educational publishers produce textbooks, supplementary reading materials, teachers' notes, exercises, digital teaching materials, audio-visual materials, tests and a wealth of other teaching and assessment aids. The content of educational publishing is geared to the needs of the curriculum, educational structure and linguistic and cultural norms of a particular national or state government.

Educational publishers often publish ELT (English Language Teaching) and EFL (English as a Foreign Language) publications as many of the same skills are required to develop materials. Oxford University Press, Cambridge University Press, McGraw Hill and Macmillan are some of the major companies in this sector.

STM, academic, scholarly and reference publishers

Some of the biggest international publishers are those that disseminate research conducted by people working in universities and research centres throughout the world. These publishers now publish primarily in digital form, although some work is still printed. Major STM (Scientific, Technical and Medical) publishers include Elsevier, Springer, John Wiley & Sons and Taylor & Francis. There are several large university presses in the UK and US that are major publishers in this sector (see case study in Chapter 6, page 160).

Publishing departments

All publishing companies have their own organizational structure, but the following gives a flavour of the way in which the departments might typically be set up, and the roles within them. All of these departments report to the Managing Director (UK); Publisher or Chief Executive Officer (CEO) are among the titles used in the US. This person is ultimately responsible to the owners or shareholders for the continued success and profitability of the company.

Editorial department

The editorial department manages the acquisition or commissioning of new publications, liaises with authors and controls the development of a project into a finished book.

- *The Editorial Director* or *Publisher* (often the same person) manages the editorial department and is responsible for the overall success of the list, and the financial viability of the publishing programme.

- *Commissioning Editors* (UK), *Acquisitions Editors* (US) or *Sponsoring Editors* (North American educational publishing) are responsible for identifying authors and developing projects with them. They play a central role in defining the development of the publisher's list, and negotiate the terms of the author-publisher contract with the author or the agent.

- *Senior Editors* in the tertiary and STM sector (also called *Publishing Editors* or *Product Managers*) manage publications in a particular subject area, such as journals, monographs, and digital resources. They work with external *Journal Editors*, *Series Editors* and other *Editorial Advisors*, drawn from academic departments and research institutes.

- *Managing Editors* look after schedules and costs, and may also manage the work of other in-house editors, freelance copy editors and proofreaders.

- *Development* or *Project Editors* work closely with the author during the writing stage to ensure that the work is progressing to schedule, in the format agreed, and to a required standard.

- *Educational* and *ELT Editors* often have teaching experience, and tend to have a hands-on approach to the development of the publishing projects under their control. Their knowledge of the curriculum and teaching practices is vital to success.

- *Production Editors* are responsible for taking the book through the design and production process, working closely with the *Production Department* (see below).

- *Copy Editors* prepare the text for production according to an agreed house style. *Proofreaders* check the work in progress for errors and omissions.

- *Picture Editors/Researchers* (often freelance) source pictures for the work, and ensure that permissions are obtained and appropriate fees negotiated.

Design and production departments

The design and production departments look after the production of printed books (p-books) and e-books, and now also often have a vital role in digital file management and digital distribution.

- The *Production Director* is in charge of this department and is ultimately responsible for all issues of production quality, schedules and cost.

- *Production Managers* and *Production Coordinators* plan and control the production process, and liaise with internal and external suppliers. Their job is to make sure that every publication is produced on schedule, at the best price and at the quality required.

- *Designers* are responsible for the visual impact and the effective use of design features in any publication. This includes page layout, cover design, use of illustrations and other non-text elements. As well as being creative, designers must work to the house style and to a brief developed to fulfil editorial and marketing requirements.

- *Production Editors* in STM or scholarly publishing may have responsibility for digital workflow from author to publication.

Marketing department

The marketing department is responsible for the branding, packaging, publicity and promotion of the firm's output, and has input into what a firm publishes.

- The *Marketing Director* is in charge of this department and is responsible for developing and protecting brand value.

- *Marketing Managers* prepare and manage campaigns for imprints, series, and individual titles. They work closely with editors preparing sales copy and providing metadata to Nielsen BookData and retailers such as Amazon.

◉ *Promotion Managers* prepare physical and digital promotion materials, such as catalogues, brochures, websites, mail and e-mail shots.

◉ *Publicity Managers* deal with the press and other media, and arrange special publicity events and author appearances.

Sales department

The sales department is responsible for ensuring the publications move profitably through the channels of distribution to the end-user.

◉ The *Sales Director* runs this department and his or her detailed knowledge of what is selling through various channels is vital to the commissioning process.

◉ *Sales Representatives* work with major trade customers, pushing new titles, negotiating special promotional deals, and handling a wide range of customer service functions.

◉ *Education, ELT* and *Academic* (UK) or *College* (US) *Representatives* visit appropriate institutions to discuss the adoption of the company's titles with teachers.

Distribution and order fulfilment

◉ The *Distribution Manager* is responsible for managing the storage and distribution of the company's publications.

◉ The *Warehouse Manager* and *Stock Controller* look after the warehouse and the company's stock of publications. As more of the company's 'stock' is in digital forms, this role is changing and is often more closely integrated with the production function.

◉ *Order Processing* or *Fulfilment Managers* handle all customer orders and make sure they are processed accurately and in a manner that leads to customer satisfaction.

◉ *Customer Services Managers* look after individual customer accounts, handle queries and complaints, and work closely with the finance department.

Finance department

The finance department looks after the company's economic affairs. It also includes the team that track sales and ensure that sales and rights income are collected when due, and that royalties to authors and commissions to sales agents are paid accurately and on time.

◉ The *Financial Director* runs the finance department. He or she is a key member of the senior management team, and ensures that individual departments prepare and keep to budgets, and manages all payments and receipts.

Chapter by chapter

Chapter 1: The fundamentals of publishing

The turbulence created by the growth of digital culture, and changes in our view of originality and creativity, mean that we need to identify the core knowledge and transferable skills required for a successful career in publishing. The global and local implications of this are placed in context through a very short history of publishing, showing how publishing today carries the legacy of technological and social developments that date back to Gutenberg's innovations in the fifteenth century.

Chapter 2: The choices publishers make

Publications come in all shapes and sizes, ranging from educational and academic to the full range of children's and adult trade books: the fiction and non-fiction books we read in our free time. These books cater for different needs and are aimed at diverse markets, and this chapter covers not only the different audiences for books and other publications, but also the different formats (print and electronic) that are now available to consumers. It also looks at how publishers apply different business models to these very different products and services.

Chapter 3: Writers, readers and intermediaries

Publishing works by making a bridge between readers and the people who create interesting stories, provide useful information or have something to teach us either in our formal education or just for fun. The authors, illustrators and other people who create what we call 'content' have a legal and moral right to control and benefit from what they have created, but they usually find it advantageous to work with others to get this material into the hands of readers. There are many people who help in this process, and this chapter looks at how agents and other gatekeepers, various networks and opinion formers can all have an important role in making sure that there is a good channel to readers, buyers and other end-users.

Chapter 4: Editorial processes

Publishers are all different and each has its own policy that defines how it decides what to publish. The publisher's list is developed according to a plan, and this usually entails publishing with a specific market niche in mind. This chapter explores how publishers acquire publishing properties and commission authors to write new publications, how editors research the market and the importance of formal and informal networks.

   The publisher must make sure that its programme is good not only for the company's reputation but also for its bottom line. The chapter also examines how the publisher/author contract is central to the publishing relationship, and explores how new formats and digital platforms are changing how publishers deal with territorial and language rights. It also looks at the process of editing a book from submission to publication, and how editors deal with other people inside and outside their own publishing organization.

Chapter 5: Design and production

Publishers have many decisions to make as there are so many formats and digital platforms for publications. Will a guidebook be better as a printed book or as an application (app) designed for iPhones, iPads or other mobile devices? How can e-books be designed for all the different e-readers on the market? What traditional print formats will be best for which markets? These are all things that require design and production skills, and the confidence and ability to project manage publications in a variety of formats for what might be widely different markets. In all this, publishers need to be constantly aware of the importance of quality in the content and form of what they are producing. They need to be able to develop and keep to realistic schedules, budget effectively and control costs, and establish pricing policies that lead to financial success. This chapter looks at how the design and production people in publishing contribute to this process.

Chapter 6: Print and electronic publishing

At a time when there are many new business models for print and electronic publishing, the market for e-books is growing rapidly; authors, agents, publishers and booksellers are choosing from a variety of media, formats and platforms. This process is being undertaken within a changing technical, legal and administrative framework. This chapter explores these changes and shows how digital workflows and software standards are developing to ensure the smooth rapid adoption of digital publishing in local and global markets.

Chapter 7: Marketing, sales and distribution

Building on the idea that all publishing is focused on satisfying a need in a target market, this chapter focuses on how all parts of the publishing organization must be aware of the eventual reader when they are acquiring, editing, designing and producing a publication. It covers sales and the supply chain to target markets, and the ways in which publishers (and authors, agents and other intermediaries) communicate through promotion, publicity and social media. These activities require publishers to be creative in developing, managing and monitoring the budgets and schedules required to put on effective marketing campaigns.

Conclusion

This book covers the origins of publishing, and shows how the work done by the many people involved with this cultural industry is changing because of the impact of digitization and globalization. Within the global media landscape, publishing still fulfils a vital cultural role in spreading ideas, information and entertainment; some of which is in print and some of which is in a widening variety of digital forms.

Additional materials

There is a wealth of material provided in appendices. Student resources include a glossary, bibliography, a list of web resources, blogs and newsletters and details of book fairs and publishers associations.

A mass-produced printed book is organized very differently from a manuscript. Title pages, dedications, contents tables, indexes, running heads, footnotes and illustrations all affect the way in which we read. The modes of classification that were stabilized by printing-house convention paved the way for the encyclopaedic mentality of the Enlightenment.'

Jonathan Bate, 'The first great age of the book',
New Statesman, *October 2011*

The
fundamentals
of publishing

Whether you are starting a publishing course, setting off on a career in publishing, or are just curious about what is going on in the publishing world, you cannot escape the fact that publishing is a cultural industry in a state of flux. The daily activities and responsibilities of everyone working in books, journals and magazines have changed significantly in the twenty-first century, and in recent years these changes have accelerated with each new technical and commercial consequence of the digital revolution.

Whatever these shifts and changes may bring to book publishing in the next decades, certain fundamentals are likely to remain central to what it means to be a publisher. Understanding these fundamentals will be vital to your success as you develop your publishing career.

A very short history of publishing

1.1
Illuminated manuscript, c. 1400
Illuminated manuscripts are considered to be among the first books. They were handwritten and heavily illustrated mainly by monastic scribes in Europe from the period after 1100. This illustration shows the baptism of Charles VI of France from *Les Grandes Chroniques de St Denis.*

We can understand most things better if we know something about their historical context. How and why has publishing developed the way it has? What are some of the critical elements that run through all publishing and how might these help us to make sense of the changes taking place today? This book cannot provide a comprehensive history of publishing (although publishing history is a fascinating field in itself and you can find pointers to further information in the Resources section at the end of this book). There are, however, some important historical details to bear in mind as you learn about the profession and find out more about publishing.

1.2

1.3

1.2
Gutenberg Bible, 1456
Printing from wood and bronze blocks had existed in Korea and China since the ninth century, but in the 1450s the Latin Bible produced by Johannes Gutenberg from Mainz in Germany was the first mass-produced printed book in Europe. Before that, each book had to be copied by hand. Several examples of the Gutenberg Bible survive.

1.3
Canterbury Tales, c. 1476
Expert analysis of the paper and the type suggests that the first edition of the *Canterbury Tales* was from 1476. As this edition does not have a preface and does not mention noble sponsors, as the printer/publisher William Caxton often did, it is possible that this publication was a commercial enterprise rather than sponsored.

Printing and publishing

There were books before the invention of printing, but there was no publishing. Texts had been written and copied by hand for religious and secular purposes for several thousand years, but publishing (the mechanical and digital reproduction and distribution of identical copies of written or illustrated works), has a history of just over 550 years. Although wooden, clay and metal moveable type had previously been used in China and Korea, Johannes Gutenberg's development of metal moveable type alongside the printing press and use of oil-based inks represents the beginning of modern publishing. From the 1450s onwards, first in Europe and then spreading across the world, publishing developed as an important agent of cultural, political, religious and social change.

The religious, philosophical and scientific movements that spread from Europe after the fifteenth century were to a large extent made possible because ideas could be written, reproduced and distributed in published works, whether they were books, journals, newspapers, pamphlets or simple broadsheets. Publishing increasingly meant the production and distribution of texts in the vernacular language (the language actually spoken by the people) rather than in the religious languages of Latin and Greek. William Caxton's successful publication of Chaucer's *Canterbury Tales* in the 1470s is an early example of publishing in English.

Typesetting

Gutenberg's typesetting was not the first; the Chinese had produced printed books since the ninth century, but it was very difficult to typeset in Chinese because of the vast number of characters required to produce a printed text. On the other hand, moveable type could more readily be used for Latin, Greek and Cyrillic alphabets, which have a smaller number of letters.

Arabic fonts were developed in sixteenth-century Europe, but typesetting in the Arabic alphabet using moveable type was not fully developed until the nineteenth century.

1.4
Non-Latin typefaces
Thanks to the Information Technology (IT) and Internet revolution, most alphabets used across the world are now available as useable fonts: these include Chinese and Japanese (see below), Korean, Thai, Bengali, Farsi, Hmong, Amharic and Inuktitut.

1.5
Typesetting with moveable type
Moveable type is stored in a compartmentalized wooden box. The typesetter selects letters and assembles them into words on a composing stick. These short sections are put together in a form or forme, and used for printing. The type in the stick is a mirror image of the text that will eventually appear on the printed page.

1.4

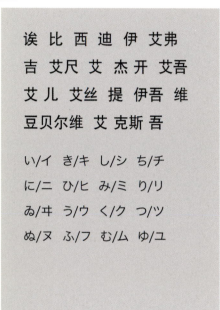

1.5

Using images

From an early date, printed publications also contained illustrations, and the use of both words and images to spread knowledge and ideas became a major element in cultural, social, economic and political discourse. The profound power of words and images to influence the way in which people interpret their lives and societies remains just as strong in our times, where digital technologies have now added to the range of ways we can create publications and reproduce and distribute text and images.

Publishing and the history of control

Just as sovereign states in the twenty-first century may monitor and try to control the transmission of ideas through digital communications, so the power of the printed word and image was soon recognized after the invention of printing. Then, as now, church and state sometimes sought to control the spread of ideas and to prevent publication of texts that were considered to be a threat to orthodoxy.

An early example of such control was the *Index Librorum Prohibitorum*, a list of publications prohibited by the Catholic Church, which lasted in various forms from 1559 until Pope Paul VI abolished it in 1966. This list was used against what were called immoral and heretical works, and also against the works of scientists such as Kepler and Galileo. Jean-Paul Sartre and Simone de Beauvoir were two prominent twentieth-century intellectuals whose books were proscribed by the *Index*.

In the course of the sixteenth century, European governments (notably in Britain and France) also acted to try and control the spread of ideas through publishing, by using censorship and restricting the ownership of printing presses.

In Europe and North America, freedom of expression was established as a cornerstone of publishing during the seventeenth and eighteenth centuries, and enshrined in the American Bill of Rights. The First Amendment to the US Constitution states: 'Congress shall make no law respecting an establishment of religion, or prohibiting the free exercise thereof; or abridging the freedom of speech, or of the press; or the right of the people peaceably to assemble, and to petition the Government for a redress of grievances.' There have, however, been many occasions since then when vibrant publishing cultures have been threatened by authoritarian legislation and repressive regimes.

1.6
Nazis burning books, 1933
'Every burned book or house enlightens
the world; every suppressed or expunged
word reverberates through the earth
from side to side.'
*Ralph Waldo Emerson, American poet,
lecturer and essayist*

1.6

At the most extreme end of this suppression we have only to think of the Nazi book burnings, the suppression of writers and publishers under the Soviet regime, or the tight state control of publishing in many authoritarian countries that continues into the twenty-first century. We should also not forget that even in the US, book banning, usually influenced by extreme religious and political groups, still takes place in some states. In recent years, J.K. Rowling's *Harry Potter* titles have been charged with promoting witchcraft and banned in parts of the US.

PEN International, with its 140 centres in 101 countries, is involved with the promotion of literature, international campaigning on issues such as translation and freedom of expression, and improving access to literature at international, regional and national levels. It works on human rights issues and campaigns for free expression and against the persecution of writers and publishers. Professional associations for publishers, booksellers and librarians (such as the American Booksellers Foundation for Free Expression) are also active in combating such censorship.

Digital publishing and the flow of information via the Internet and other digital networks have created new challenges to freedom of speech. Modern communications technology makes it easier to distribute materials that challenge religious and secular authorities. However, at the same time, it gives great control to those who can influence the content of publications and limit access to materials with which they do not agree, or which they see as damaging to their political or commercial interests. While much publicity has been given to Internet censorship in some countries considered to have repressive regimes, nearly all countries keep close surveillance on Internet usage, ostensibly in the interests of national security.

Top 10 banned or challenged books for 2000–2009 (according to the American Library Association)

The majority of these publications were either banned or challenged in the US, by a mixture of schools (often prompted by parent complaints), school libraries and public libraries.

1. *Harry Potter* (series),
   by J.K. Rowling
2. *Alice* series,
   by Phyllis Reynolds Naylor
3. *The Chocolate War,*
   by Robert Cormier
4. *And Tango Makes Three,*
   by Justin Richardson/Peter Parnell
5. *Of Mice and Men,*
   by John Steinbeck
6. *I Know Why the Caged Bird Sings,* by Maya Angelou
7. *Scary Stories* (series),
   by Alvin Schwartz
8. *His Dark Materials* (series),
   by Philip Pullman
9. *ttyl; ttfn; l8r g8r* (series),
   by Lauren Myracle
10. *The Perks of Being a Wallflower,*
    by Stephen Chbosky

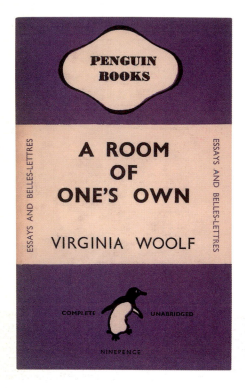

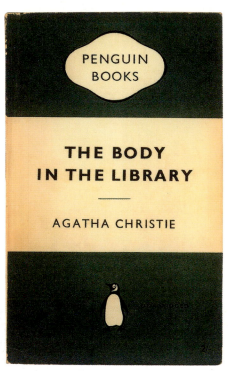

1.7
Penguin paperbacks
Featuring what
Allen Lane called the
'dignified but flippant'
penguin symbol,
the first Penguin
paperbacks appeared
in the summer of 1935
and included works
by Ernest Hemingway,
André Maurois and
Agatha Christie.
They were colour
coded (green for crime,
orange for fiction, etc.).

1.7

How buying books has changed

In the nineteenth and twentieth centuries developments in printing, paper and binding technology made it possible for publishers to vastly increase their output and the kind of publications that they could produce. Advances in education and literacy enlarged the market for published materials of all kinds. The development of urban societies, national and international transportation and communication infrastructures, and a cultural class increasingly centred on the literary culture, made publishing a central part of civil society. During this time many public and private libraries were opened, helped in many cases by funding from industrial empires like that of Andrew Carnegie, the Scottish-American steel magnate. It was also a period that saw the development of modern bookselling.

The current debate about how books are to be bought and sold is just the most recent stage of a complex history. For many years books were mainly sold to 'subscribers' who put up money before publication in order that the publisher would have the finance necessary to produce the book (in the UK, selling new books into the book trade is still sometimes referred to as 'subscription'). The publication of both fiction and non-fiction in serial and partwork form has a long history, and digital publication has led to increased interest in the idea of subscription services and to the publication of individual chapters (particularly those delivered via mobile devices).

At times book publishers have also been booksellers, printers, magazine and newspaper publishers. The changing corporate ownership of publishers in recent decades is just the latest part of this history. The current shifts caused by the effect of digital culture are part of a constant development. The fact that digital distributors, such as Amazon, have now become publishers in their own right again raises issues of whether it is a good thing for companies to control all parts of the production and supply chain – what is called 'vertical integration'.

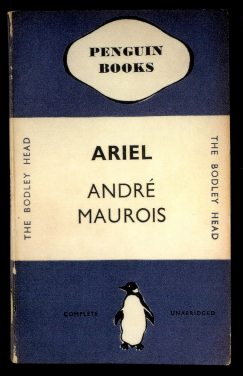

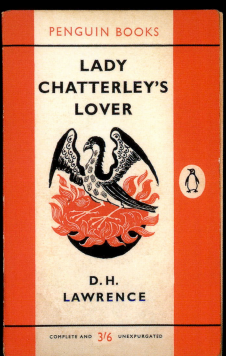

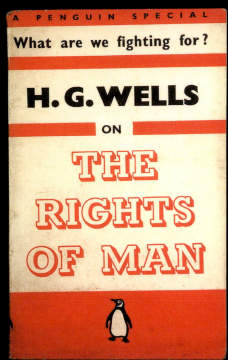

'We believed in the existence in this country of a vast reading public for intelligent books at a low price, and staked everything on it.'

Allen Lane, founder of Penguin Books

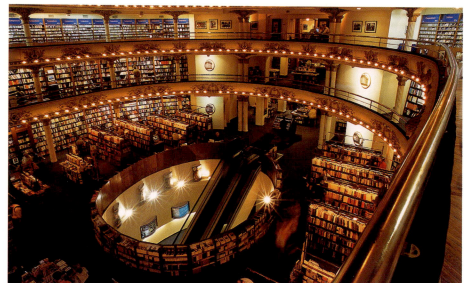

1.8

1.8
El Ateneo bookstore, Buenos Aires
Some bookstores, such as El Ateneo in Buenos Aires, Selexyz Dominicanen bookstore in Maastricht, McNally-Jackson in New York, and Daunt Books in London are becoming 'destination shops', making the most of their stunning premises and their traditional focus on customer experience.

Early booksellers

Early booksellers were often also printers and publishers, and bookselling as we know it today really stems from the late nineteenth and early twentieth century. Foyles of London was founded in 1903, Barnes and Noble's first bookshop was opened in New York in 1917 (although they had been publishing since 1873), and Gibert in Paris moved to retail premises in 1888 after two years as a *bouquiniste*, selling books from a stall on the side of the River Seine.

Outside Europe, bookshops frequently developed as stationers, publishers of government and educational publications and sellers of religious texts. The long histories of companies such as Higginbothams of Madras (founded 1844) and Angus and Robertson of Sydney (founded 1884) point to the importance of the written culture in the Imperial Age, when European powers controlled much of the world.

The development of railways led to a new sort of publishing and bookselling, with Penguin books apocryphally being created after Allen Lane found nothing good to read at the kiosk while waiting for a train at Exeter station in 1935. Station book kiosks prospered throughout Europe in the twentieth century, with Narvesen in Norway being an early example of a bookselling outlet publishing specific titles for the travelling public. The paperback market was greatly expanded after the Second World War (with a readership that had become familiar with reading paperback fiction in Special Armed Services Editions (US) and the UK Books for the Forces programme), with the first WH Smith shop opening at Euston station in London in 1848.

Post-1945 publishing in the US saw the growth of companies such as Pocket Books, Dell, Avon and Harlequin. Also catering for the travelling masses, airport bookshops developed in the late twentieth century as a major outlet for trade publishers.

Book-buying options

The bookselling world has gone through a number of structural changes in recent decades. In the US, there was the growth and then decline of the multi-chain mall bookshops. This was followed by the growth of other book chains, such as Borders (which went out of business in 2011). These chains brought lifestyle marketing (comfortable sofas and coffee shops) to the US retail book business, a trend that was soon followed in Europe and Asia.

The entry of the major supermarket chains into bookselling (most notably Walmart in the US, and Tesco in the UK) brought about further changes in buying habits, increasing demand for the type of titles that they stock. This affected trade publishers' margins, as the supermarkets continued the trend the book chains had started, and pushed publishers to increase their discounts.

The supermarkets sold books at low prices (often as loss leaders) to their customers, and altered the perception of some consumers about the value of books. This has left a legacy, with consumers expecting e-books to be free or very cheap.

The dominance of online booksellers (also big discounters) has not yet led to the death of the traditional bookstore. Bricks-and-mortar bookshops are finding ways (often in collaboration with book wholesalers) to compete on the sale of e-books, print-on-demand (POD) publications and independently published books.

The issue of fixed prices for e-books is subject to recent decisions in several European countries, as is the low- or zero-rate VAT (sales tax) that has been applied to print books but is not being applied to e-books in all cases. As is often the case, the law is having to catch up with the possibilities of technology as books move around the globe unencumbered by the territorial restrictions entailed in most publishing agreements.

Pricing

All publications must be priced at a level that is acceptable to the purchaser, and provide the author, publisher and bookseller with sufficient income to cover their expenses and produce a profit. You should be aware right from the beginning that pricing issues are a central concern in all parts of the industry. Pricing issues are often complicated because of national and international regulations, which developed to deal with trade in physical publications, before the cross-border trade in intangible digital goods was even imagined. Examples of this are fixed price regulations in many countries, under which publishers establish a price that must be charged by all retailers, with discounts to customers allowed in very rare specific circumstances. Such a sytem existed in the UK under the Net Book Agreement until the 1990s, and still exists in France under the *Loi Lang*.

Print-on-demand (POD)

POD technology uses digital files that make it possible for single copies of books to be produced in response to individual orders. Some new books and many backlist titles are now produced using POD, which has made it possible for more titles to be published and kept in print, so that they remain available to customers worldwide. Customers do not have to wait for reprints, and the costs of warehousing and distribution are reduced. POD has also made it easier for small publishers to start up as they do not have to invest capital in stocks of books.

Discussion questions

1. What made publishing 'as we know it today' possible?

2. Do you think publishing is a central part of a civilized society?

3. How did the changes in bookselling help to increase book-buying options?

4. What is POD? Do you think it will make a major impact on the future of the industry? Which kinds of publishing might benefit most from POD technology?

The relationship between different parts of the industry

Publishing firms, like most industries in the last 50 or so years, have changed through a process of conglomeration, acquisition, productive (and unproductive) mergers, internationalization and globalization, technical innovation, marketing revolutions and development of brand identities. The relationship of publishers to other actors in the publishing process (authors, agents, booksellers) has continued to develop, often through periods of conflict and disagreement, and publishers have had to understand and adapt to developments coming from other industries, other media and, most notably, the IT and communication sectors.

Understanding the book chain

Publishing corporations have grown and diversified, and at the same time new companies have emerged. These have produced innovations in either their approach to newly identified market niches and new sales and distribution channels, production techniques and innovative formats, or the emergence of new economic and business models.

In particular, the period since 2000 has been a time of change due to the rise of new media platforms, social media, print-on-demand, self-publishing, and the interactive media and games industries. The publishing world is embracing the possibilities of these new technologies.

The publisher's role as intermediary between the creators and consumers of content has always meant that the relationships that a publisher has with other members of the 'book chain' are central to the publisher's success. It is important that the publisher is successful in marketing itself to both the creators and the consumers of its publications. As we will see in Chapter 3, there are many people involved in the networks that connect the various components of the publishing process; but before looking at this complexity in detail (and how it is changing) it's a good idea to think about the fundamentals of these relationships.

Firstly, as you start to develop your publishing career, you should think about how you deal with other people at a professional level. It is important that you treat people with respect and consideration, be prepared to learn from the experience of others and to pass on things you have learnt to colleagues. While there have traditionally been many larger-than-life characters in publishing, most people take up a career in publishing because they have a feeling for words and images, believe in the power of communication, value the creativity of the human spirit, and are generally curious about other people.

Secondly, publishing relies on a belief that accuracy and integrity are important. Good publishers do not like sloppy editing or low production standards. Nor do they like authors who plagiarize, people who produce unauthorized pirated copies of copyright protected works, or publications that gratuitously offend human sensibilities or human rights. They do, however, realize that the expression of views that may go against established thinking is one of the purposes of publishing. Your relationships with others will be stronger if you understand this from the beginning.

In addition, you will not be an effective publisher unless you have a good understanding of the roles of the people and organizations that you have to deal with on a regular basis. (There is a section on the different jobs people do on pages 8–11.) Your publishing career will be greatly enhanced by developing a broad knowledge of all parts of the publishing process. Understanding who does what and how they do it will help you to do your job, and this includes all the major functions within a publishing company: from editorial to design; from typography to print production management; from publicity to sales and distribution. It also includes both physical and digital production methods; marketing through personal as well as digital networks; and business models that rely on a range of revenue sources. These vary from the sale of printed publications to subscription and pay-per-use, with advertising-based models used by many newspapers and magazines.

1.9

1.9
Kindle
At the last stage of the book chain, when the finished publication ends up in a reader's hands, e-books and p-books compete for market share, with the Kindle playing a major role.

As you progress through your publishing career you are likely to find that you specialize in at least one area of expertise. Your learning will never be over. The context of publishing, changes in global economic structures and relationships, the never-ending acceleration of technological change will require you to develop a personal lifelong learning strategy.

Discussion questions

1. How has publishing changed in the past 50 years? How might it change in the next 50 years?

2. What makes an effective publisher? Does publishing attract a certain kind of person? If so, why might this be?

3. Why do publishers need to pay attention to detail? There are obvious reasons for editorial staff, but which other roles need precision and meticulous planning?

4. Why is it important to understand what other people do in their jobs? Which departments need to work particularly closely, and why?

Preparing for a future in publishing

As you are reading this book you may already work in publishing or have decided to explore the possibilities of publishing as a career. Your background, current skills, and your personal inclinations and ambitions will play a part as you make a choice to specialize in editorial or production work, rights sales and administration, marketing and promotion, sales and distribution or finance and business management. These will be covered as you work your way through *The Publishing Business*, but there are some things that are so important to all publishing that we will examine them now.

Attention to detail

People have an expectation when they read or refer to any published work, whether this is a leather-bound tome or a mobile app. We expect something that is 'published' to be accurate, consistent and reliable in a way that we may not expect of a casual conversation, a piece of printed propaganda, a website geared to selling us a particular product or service, or any other of the unattributed sources available in print, through multimedia channels or online.

Publishers have a responsibility to make sure that writers have appropriate specialist knowledge and must check the truth of anything that is to be published as 'fact'. Then the reader can feel confident that the information and views contained in the publication can be trusted. This is something that has become more difficult as the cultural balance has shifted toward celebrating democratic, open participation rather than honouring deep specialist knowledge and accuracy.

Publishers also need to make sure that any published material is consistent in terms of the terminology it uses, the reading level required, the use of language, and the physical layout and organization of the text and illustrations. Publishers generally select writers because of their specialist knowledge and their ability to express themselves in an engaging and consistent way, but the ultimate responsibility for making sure the author's work is useful and attractive to the reader will always lie with the publisher. This is much more than just checking spelling. It means that publishers must always pay attention to detail, and this applies not only in the work that editors do to ensure the reliability and accessibility of the text. It also applies to the designers and production staff, marketing and promotion teams and to the sales and distribution departments.

Respect for the creator

Just as attention to detail shows a respect for the readers' needs and expectations, everyone in publishing needs to understand the rights and expectations of the authors, illustrators and other creators whose hard work and trust is essential to any successful publication.

The formal relationship between the author and the publisher is determined by a contract or letter of agreement.

The main purpose of the contract between the publisher and the author (the word 'author' is frequently used to mean anyone who creates a work) is to specify what rights the author is granting to the publisher. The rights granted will usually be 'volume rights' – the right to publish the text in book form in any format in any language throughout the world. Subsidiary rights to publish in particular territories, particular languages or in particular formats (paperback, e-book, etc.) may then be sublicensed to other publishers.

The contract determines how the economic benefits of publication will be shared between the author and the publisher. The contract is based on the copyright law of the country specified in the contract (we will explore these aspects of contract and copyright in later chapters), and the relationship between the author and the publisher must also take into account other, non-economic, matters that are also fundamental to publishing.

Moral rights and copyright

The copyright laws of many countries now specifically cover what are known as 'moral rights', and in the European context these include the right of the author to be identified as the creator; the author's right to have his or her work published properly, without unwarranted or sloppy editing or production qualities (the right of integrity); the author's right to be identified as the creator of a work, not being falsely attributed to someone else (right of attribution); and certain privacy rights.

As well as these legal requirements, and possibly of equal importance, is the need for publishers to develop good professional relationships with authors. This will entail the common human decencies, such as respect for cultural difference, zero tolerance of racism and sexism, and an acknowledgement that there is a common interest shared by author and publisher in producing publications that are useful and valuable to their readers.

UK copyright is governed by the Copyright, Designs and Patents Act 1988, which specifies that the length of copyright protection is 70 years from the end of the calendar year in which the last remaining author of the work dies. This is in line with European Union Copyright.

US copyright protection also lasts for 70 years and is governed by title 17 of the United States Code, including amendments.

Copyright in other parts of the world is the responsibility of national governments, most of whom are also signatories to the Berne Convention, which requires its signatories to recognize the copyright of works of authors from other signatory countries (known as members of the Berne Union) in the same way as it recognizes the copyright of its own nationals. The World Intellectual Property Organization provides a useful guide to the complexities of international copyright law.

'… what is missing more and more from today's publishing environment is the demand for and insistence on quality editing.'

Woll, T., 2010. Publishing for Profit. *4th ed.*
Chicago: Chicago Review Press

Awareness of audiences

Publishing is by its very definition intended to distribute an entertaining, informative or educational work to an audience that wants or needs what the publication contains. Authors, literary agents, scouts, commissioning editors, marketing managers, promotion and publicity experts, and many others working with publishers, authors and booksellers have views on who wants what sort of book, and how much they expect to pay. While in some instances the role of a specialized market research department will be critical in determining the publishing direction of a particular publishing firm, everyone in the organization can have a valuable view of what might sell to a particular audience.

No publication will exist for long without readers, and you will need to work throughout your career to understand what people want to read, how they want to read, why they will want to read – and much more besides. However, it is also important to remember that sometimes books take many years to find an audience. For example *Moby Dick* by Herman Melville was certainly not an instant success when it first published in 1851 – receiving mixed critical reviews, before becoming established as one of the great American novels.

Discussion questions

1. What is the main purpose of the contract between publisher and creator?

2. What are moral rights?

3. What is the difference between moral rights and copyright?

4. How might you start researching a new subject and market? What tools would you need?

The global and local fundamentals

At a global level, publishing companies serve readers with a wide variety of publications. Some publishing enterprises are quite large and some are part of major media corporations. Their operations are governed by the need to provide shareholders with good returns on their investment. These companies frequently have a global reach, and they have acquired companies or formed joint ventures in many promising new markets. At the other end of the scale, some publishers are very small, often one individual or a small group, doing it more for the love than for the money. In between, there are medium-sized independent publishers such as Canongate, Faber and Faber and Workman Publishing.

Major corporations

Internationally there were 20 publishers with a turnover of over a billion US dollars in 2010. Of these, the top ten demonstrate the dominance of publishing groups with headquarters in the North Atlantic Region (four from US/Canada, and six from Europe). In descending order, they are Pearson, Reed Elsevier, Thomson Reuters, Wolters Kluwer, Bertelsmann, Hachette Livre, McGraw-Hill Education, Grupo Planeta, Cengage Learning and Scholastic.

These ten organizations represent different types of publishing and include many of the better-known publishing brands and publishing imprints, as can be seen in the following five brief company profiles.

◉ **Pearson** (more than $8 billion) (more than £5 billion) focuses on education through Prentice Hall, Addison-Wesley and Longmans, and Pearson Education is a major force in the US. The Penguin Group and its many imprints are active publishers in English-speaking countries and China. The Business Information Group (including the *Financial Times*) is a global leader in financial information.

◉ **Wolters Kluwer** (nearly $5 billion) (nearly £3.2 billion) provides information on finance, tax, law, business and health. It publishes for the professional market using a wide variety of media including online reference materials, journals, books, software and loose-leaf services.

1.10

1.10
London Book Fair
At book fairs, publishers discuss industry developments, and introduce new publishing projects. This seminar on children's books in translation is typical of the many discussions that take place each year at the London Book Fair.

◉ **Lagardère** (nearly $3 billion) (nearly £1.90 billion) is a French conglomerate that includes Hachette companies worldwide. Lagardère also publishes under imprints such as Larousse, Grasset, Édition Dunod and Les Éditions Albert René.

◉ **Grupo Planeta** (over $2 billion) (over £1.3 billion) is the biggest Spanish publisher. It publishes for Spain and Latin America and also owns a major French publishing group, Editis. Planeta has more than 100 publishing imprints, some of which are gathered under the Grup 62 banner. Famous Planeta imprints include Seix Barral, Emecé Editores, Austral and Deusto in Spain, and Bordas, Belfond, and Univers Poche in France There are Planeta companies throughout Latin America.

◉ **Cengage Learning** (over $2 billion) (over £1.3 billion) is a major US-based supplier of educational publications in the US and worldwide. It has an extensive network of international business partners, and has expanded its activities significantly in China. As well as publishing for schools, universities and vocational courses, Cengage also has an extensive reference publishing programme. Cengage owns Brooks/Cole, Wadsworth and South-Western, vocational publisher Delmar, and Gale, one of the world's major publishers of reference materials for libraries. In Heinle, it has a major educational and ELT imprint, and it acquired Nelson Thornes in 2011.

Territories

For many years publishers have divided the world into different sales territories in which they have exclusive or non-exclusive rights to sell their edition of a work. These sales territories are based on historical areas of influence, and political and cultural affinity. British publishers have tended to retain rights to sell their editions in the UK and the British Commonwealth, and the territorial rights of the American publisher to the same book would include the US, Canada and other territories closely associated with the US. Over time these traditional territorial rights have been challenged in the courts on the basis that they restrain trade.

The most translated authors

According to the United Nations Educational, Scientific and Cultural Organization (UNESCO), the world's top five most translated authors are:

◉ Agatha Christie (7,006 translations)
◉ Jules Verne (4,589 translations)
◉ William Shakespeare (4,043 translations)
◉ Enid Blyton (3,710 translations)
◉ Vladimir Lenin (3,506 translations)

Source: Index Translationum, UNESCO

Other issues involve changes in global trading patterns, US and EU competition law (allowing for some elements of differential pricing from jurisdiction to jurisdiction), changes in copyright law (as in Australia where the rules on copyright protection for books imported from outside Australia have been subject to review), and the use of new publishing media (which may or may not be subject to sales taxes and custom tariffs at the same rate as physical publications). If the sale and distribution of a 'book', 'magazine' or 'newspaper' now means downloading or accessing a digital file, many of the controls that could be placed on the physical movement of goods are irrelevant. But this does not mean the end of regulation. New ways of limiting the sale of e-books in territories are being developed. The old regime of territorial rights is being adapted to the new market conditions, but it is now increasingly language rather than geography that determines the limits of a given market.

Many more territories are now 'open markets', meaning that any edition can be sold into the market. For British and American publishers this means that different editions of the same title compete in world markets, and the sale and distribution of books via the Internet (in both physical and digital forms) has made it far more difficult for publishers to monitor which editions of which publications get into the hands (or onto the e-reading devices) of which customers.

Language

Publishing is both a local and an international business. The language of publication obviously determines the audience for any publication, and is related to other social and political factors that also define markets. Literary works and children's books are vital to the healthy development of any language. Just as people speak and read many different languages, so publishing around the world reflects the diversity of human knowledge and expression.

Books are usually written in one language for a specific market and may then be made available to readers in other markets in either the original language or in translated form. Some types of books, particularly popular fiction and children's books, are widely translated.

English is now the dominant language of science and business, and this is likely to remain the case. But this does not mean that the UK and US will continue to dominate publishing in science and business. A report by the Royal Society (*Knowledge, Networks and Nations: Global scientific collaboration in the 21st century*) predicted that China would overtake the US in terms of English-language science publication by 2013, with India, Brazil, Iran, Tunisia and Turkey also having a large impact.

Could Mandarin or Urdu become the major publishing languages of the future? Some think so, and point to the fact that Latin, French, German and English have all had their periods of dominance, related to the political outreach of the countries that used those languages. This is equally true of the languages used on the Internet. While the World Wide Web was initially dominated by English, this is no longer the case, and Mandarin, Spanish, Japanese, Korean, Portuguese, Persian, Russian and Arabic are now all big online languages – and are growing.

School textbooks are usually intended for a local market determined by the implementation of a national or regional curriculum. Professional accounting and legal publications have content that relates to a particular jurisdiction. Many publications that cover local history, customs, food, music and literature have a market restricted to a particular region (and tourists visiting that region). In many parts of the world, regional publishing, in languages such as Samí or Welsh, is part of a lively culture and is often supported by local governments and not-for-profit cultural bodies.

However, many of the major companies in local markets are international corporations, which over the years have acquired specialist publishing imprints, and rights to globally recognized authors and characters, and they are often interwoven with other media companies that help in the promotion of publications and developments in other media.

'So many books! So little time!'

It used to be relatively easy to track the number of books published in a given territory each year, and approximate totals are still published by publishing organizations. However, in recent years this has become a much more problematic task. It is no longer possible to count the number of new ISBNs (the unique identifier allocated to each edition of a book) to get a reasonably reliable annual estimate of the number of new publications. The explosion of publishing in different formats, means that a single book might be assigned multiple ISBNs to cover all its different iterations.

The picture is made even more confused as individual chapters and sections are available as downloads or apps, and publishers republish public domain works (those where the copyright period has expired) and out-of-print materials. In addition, a total count of publishing output might now also include blogs, social media pages, and computer games that have many book-like features, and pamphlets printed by small organizations and self-publishing individuals.

International author brands

The author of a book is one of its most distinguishing features, and some authors are international brands. In trade publishing we are familiar with the selling power of authors such as John Grisham and Dan Brown, and this is true in many mass-market genres such as romance (think of Catherine Cookson and Barbara Cartland), thrillers (Robert Ludlum and James Patterson), bodice rippers (Jackie Collins and Danielle Steel), or Westerns (Zane Grey and Louis L'Amour).

Authors of literary fiction also have significant, and increasingly international, brand value. If you walk the halls of the London Book Fair or Book Expo in New York you can see the works (and photographs) of the same authors at the stands of publishers from around the world. Ian McEwan, Jonathan Franzen, Amélie Nothomb, Haruki Murakami, Wole Soyinka, Gabriel García Márquez are all global literary figures with strong 'brand' images and following.

Children's books and books for young adults (YA) sometimes have equally strong author brands, such as Maurice Sendak, Lemony Snicket, Jacqueline Wilson and Stephanie Meyer. For younger children it is often the characters that have the upper hand: Astérix and Postman Pat are instantly recognizable to children around the world, as are classic characters such as Ratty and Toad from *Wind in the Willows*, Moomintroll, and Winnie the Pooh.

Branding in other areas can also be an important factor in creating customer loyalty and global readership. The creators of graphic novels, manga and comic books frequently develop reader loyalty through character branding (such as Lucky Luke and Tintin) but readers are also attracted to specific authors and illustrators.

Author branding is also significant in other types of publishing. We very often refer to the textbooks we use by the author's name. Business students will read 'Kotler', and economists refer to 'Lipsey' or 'Samuelson', for example.

1.11

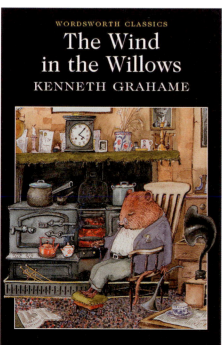

1.11
The Wind in the Willows
The characters in children's books often have international appeal. They also drive a worldwide industry that produces merchandise such as dolls, clothing, games, cards and other branded goods. This book is published by Wordsworth Editions.

Discussion questions

1. How have global trading patterns changed?

2. Does technology help or hinder publication in different languages?

3. What is an ISBN?

4. Why is author branding important?

Case study:

Bertelsmann and

Random House

Royalty payments, NSR and the agency model

Royalties to authors are not usually paid as a percentage of the list price of a book, but on the basis of the publisher's Net Sales Revenue or Receipts (NSR). This is the money received by the publisher after any discounts or commissions have been given to customers.

Under the agency model the e-bookseller usually takes 30 per cent commission on the sales price and passes the remaining 70 per cent to the publisher. Author royalties for e-book sales under the agency model are typically 25 per cent or more of the publisher's NSR.

Over the years, large media companies have bought many smaller publishing companies. The important trade publisher, Random House, was acquired by Bertelsmann, and we can learn some interesting lessons about publishing by exploring this company.

In 1835 Carl Bertelsmann founded the publishing house C. Bertelsmann Verlag in Gütersloh, Germany. During its first 100 years its main interest was theological publishing, and it was not until the 1920s that it began to publish fiction. By 1943 it was the country's top publisher in terms of book production and unit sales, but, towards the end of the war, Bertelsmann came into conflict with the Nazi power structure and was closed down.

The firm was re-established after 1945, and in 1950 Bertelsmann responded to the tough economic climate with direct-to-consumer sales that were to form the basis of a book club empire. It also expanded by acquiring a number of media companies, and took major steps to develop its international publishing business in the 1980s. With the acquisition of Random House in 1998, Bertelsmann became one of the world's most powerful publishing businesses. Random House publishes some of the major writers of contemporary fiction.

In recent years Random House has come into conflict with other parts of the publishing world, illustrating some of the ways in which e-book development has brought about the need for changes to business practice.

The role of literary agents

In 2010 Random House had a well-publicized battle with prominent literary agent Andrew Wylie about whether or not he had the right to control e-book rights for the authors that he represented. The issue came to a head when Wylie claimed that Random House needed to negotiate (and pay) separately for the right to produce e-books of backlist titles for which they had book publishing contracts. The arrival of the new medium of e-books required a new legal arrangement and Random House and Wylie eventually agreed terms. This was an important milestone in setting up e-book rights as a new right, and it helped to establish industry standards in relation to the future development of the e-book market.

The agency model

In 2011 Random House was the last major publisher to change to the 'agency model' in pricing e-books for sale through e-booksellers. Under this model, publishers set the price and e-booksellers act as agents for them. The agency model also means that retailers such as Amazon are not able to offer publisher's books at 'loss-leader' prices, something that they had used to promote the sale of their reading devices. Publishers set higher prices for e-books than those set by Amazon, which is good for the publishers, their authors and independent retailers (unless of course it pushes readers towards illegal editions).

Random House's decision consolidated a business practice and influenced Amazon and Kobo to become publishers in their own right, meaning they could set their own prices. For this reason, and possible legal challenges, the agency model is being re-evaluated.

International

Random House is the world's largest English-language general trade book publisher. It grew from the original American company to embrace Canada (1944), and the UK (1987) by acquiring Chatto, Virago, Bodley Head and Jonathan Cape, Century Hutchinson (1989), and the trade division of Reed Books (1997). When Bertelsmann purchased Random House in 1998, the imprints included Doubleday, Bantam Books, Knopf, Vintage, Ballantine and Transworld. The company now has subsidiaries in Australia, New Zealand, South Africa and India.

Bertelsmann Divisions

TV and radio; media services; press; direct marketing; and book publishers. Bertelsmann AG operates in over 50 countries, has over 100,000 employees, and has revenues of over €15 billion (approx. £12.5 billion/$20 billion), which in 2010 were divided as follows: RTL Group: 34.7%; Arvato: 31.5%; Gruner + Jahr: 15.8%; Direct Group: 6.6%; Random House: 11.4%.

TV (Europe)	RTL	TV stations in 10 European countries.
Media and communications services	Arvato Services	Printing, finance and mobile services, in over 30 countries worldwide.
Newspapers and magazines	Gruner + Jahr	285 print titles in over 20 countries, and professional websites. Printing plants in Germany and the US.
Retail	DirectGroup Bertelsmann	Media clubs, bookstores, Internet, publishing and distribution.

Publishing: Random House

More than 11,000 new books issued a year and 500 million books sold annually, makes Random House the largest general-interest book publisher.

Authors include: Bill Bryson, J.M. Coetzee, Ildefonso Falcones, Al Gore, John Grisham, John Irving, Dean Koontz, Nigella Lawson, Cormac McCarthy, Ian McEwan, Julia Navarro, Orhan Pamuk, and John Updike.

Publishing houses: Nearly 200 independent imprints in 19 countries, including Alfred A. Knopf (US); Transworld (UK); Plaza & Janés Editores S.A. (Spain); Editorial Sudamericana (Argentina) and Goldmann (Germany).

Employees: 5,264 (as of December 31, 2010)

Revenues: €1.8 billion (approx. £1.5 billion/$2.5 billion) (fiscal year 2010)

Key points

The way in which large publishing companies react to changes in the competitive environment can be critical for both their own successful development and for the way in which the industry as a whole develops. The Random House case shows the following:

◉ **Adaptability**: Bertelsmann adapted and changed its business at several times in its history in response to political, economic, social and technology changes (the so-called PEST factors). These factors were taken into account when Bertelsmann acquired Random House.

◉ **'Oil tanker' effect**: Larger established companies are not usually the first to react to change. The 'oil tanker' effect (a figure of speech referring to the time it takes to change direction in a very large vessel) meant that Random House took time to develop a strategy to deal with the new business relationships brought about by the rise of e-books.

◉ **Impact of large companies**: When Random House management did take a stand on its relationship with other parts of the publishing industry (in this case agents and e-booksellers) the effect was significant in consolidating changes to which others had already either adapted, or for which they had fought in vain.

◉ **Agency model**: By agreeing to follow the lead of the other major publishers, Random House's decision to embrace the agency model consolidated a business practice that became well established. It also had a major influence in persuading e-book retailers such as Amazon and Kobo to become publishers in their own right – so that they could set their own prices.

◉ **Internationalization**: Random House is an international company, and is not generally identified as either German or American. It has, however, chosen to focus on its pre-eminence in publishing in the English language, although it does now have some local language publishing programmes, particularly in the larger emerging markets of Asia and Latin America. Random House's international reach is important in securing global English-language rights to major authors' work in a market environment where borders are increasingly porous for both printed books and those delivered through digital channels.

Activity

Research one of the other large publishing groups, for example, Hachette, HarperCollins, Pan Macmillan, Penguin Group or Simon & Schuster.

1. Investigate the corporate structure of your chosen publishing group and compare it with Bertelsmann.

2. How does your chosen publishing house compare with Bertelsmann in terms of its international companies?

3. What different imprints does your chosen publishing group have, and how have they evolved in recent years?

4. Has the company made any significant acquisitions?

5. Which international markets are particularly important for the company?

6. What significant innovations has the company made in terms of its digital publishing strategy?

The choices publishers make

Publications come in all shapes and sizes, ranging from educational and academic to the full range of children's and adult trade books: fiction and non-fiction. All books are published with the goal of satisfying some need, whether this is a desire to be entertained, a search for information, to pursue formal or informal education, for our hobbies and personal relationships, or for spiritual and moral guidance. Remember that two of the most widely read books in the world are the Bible and the Koran.

This chapter examines how publishers produce books and other publications for different audiences, and explores the various formats (print and electronic) that are used to make these publications available to diverse market sectors. It also takes a preliminary look at how the publishing business aims to make a profit.

Varieties of publication – markets and audiences

Traditional publishers have increased their output enormously in the decade after 2000: in the UK, for example, output of new titles increased from 63,807 in 2000 to 151,969 in 2010 (Publishers Association). Output in many other countries has also expanded, and throughout the world new entrants have added to an enormous blossoming of physical and digital publishing by organizations, special interest groups, and self publishers. The chart below shows some key statistics on book output in 2010.

Book output in 2010			
Country	Book market size 2010	New titles per year 2010	Estimated e-book percentage 2010
US	$27,940 million	950,000 (including e-books)	6.2%
UK	£3,100 million	151,969	6%
Germany	€9,691 million	93,124	1%
France	€5,600 million	66,595	1.8%
Spain	€2,890 million	80,000	3.4%
Italy	€3,408 million	58,829	N/A
Sweden	SEK2,292 million	4,077	N/A
The Netherlands	€1,168 million	21,337	1.2%
Slovenia	€90 million	6,139	N/A
Poland	€697 million	21,740	N/A
Brazil	€1,352 million	52,510	N/A
China	€8,200 million	168,296	N/A

Statistical sources: IPA; National Publishers Associations; The Future of eBooks, 2011; The Global eBook Market

How do publishers decide what to publish and how to publish? And how are business models changing to make sure that publishing remains a sustainable activity?

Publishing seeks to satisfy the needs and expectations of a group of readers, the market that the author and publisher have identified in the course of developing the publishing project. Different publishing categories are one of the bases on which publishing is organized. Within each category there is a constant search for new market niches (groups of people with similar interests and needs) to which suitable publications can be directed.

Publishing categories, formats and distribution channels	
Category	Trade: Adult fiction, adult non-fiction, children and young adults (YA), religion, reference Non-trade: Education, academic, professional, scholarly
Format	Physical: Hardcover, paperback, mass-market, audio Non-physical: Audio, e-books, enhanced e-books, m-books (books for mobile phones), apps for mobile devices
Channel	Retail stores: Chains, independents, mass merchants, speciality stores, and stores at stations and airports Other channels: Online retail, downloads, direct-to-consumer, institutional sales, book clubs and fairs, export sales, jobbers and wholesalers

2.1
Harry Potter
The *Harry Potter* series of books has been produced in many different editions. Some, like these with the photos on the covers, were packaged especially for adult readers (photos by Michael Wildsmith). The covers for the Signature boxed set were created by the artist Clare Melinsky for Bloomsbury Publishing.

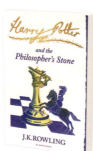

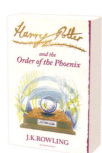

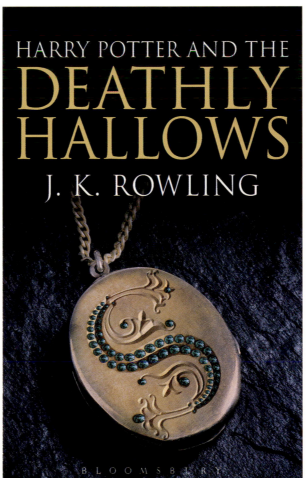

2.1

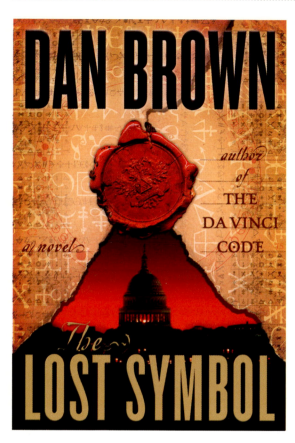

2.2
The Lost Symbol
Dan Brown's books
are a regular feature
on bestseller lists.
They are published in
52 languages around
the world with 200
million copies in print.
The Lost Symbol is a
follow-up to *The Da
Vinci Code* – one of the
bestselling novels of
all time. To reinforce
the importance of the
author's brand, his
name is given equal
weighting with the
book's title. This
edition is published
by Random House.

Trade publishing

Trade books are the fiction and non-fiction books that we read in our spare time and that are sold or distributed through bookstores, online retailers, libraries and wholesalers. They are also known as general or consumer books. Fiction includes novels and stories of all kinds, and non-fiction covers a wide variety of categories such as biography, popular history, cookery books and travel writing. We usually read these books for pleasure or to help us with other leisure activities. Other than children's books, fiction titles usually contain just the text of the story, while non-fiction books often contain illustrations, charts, maps and photographs.

Trade titles are most likely to be advertised on posters, television and in magazines. Because they are often impulse purchases, publishers generally use specific design elements to appeal to their target readers. The cover or dust jacket design is used to attract customers, along with blurbs and recommendations printed on the front and back covers.

The authors of trade books may be celebrities, specialists or people well known to the public through their appearances in other media. Some books, aimed at the general consumer, sell in very large numbers, although such books are rare. Nevertheless, publishers make huge efforts to promote their books in the hope that they will become bestsellers, and are generally satisfied when sales reach the level required to cover costs and produce some profit. This requires a well-coordinated publicity and promotion campaign, as the window of opportunity to create a bestseller in an increasingly crowded media landscape is now weeks rather than months.

Children's publishing

The characters in children's books can become world famous brands such as *The Cat in a Hat*, *Paddington Bear*, *The Hungry Caterpillar*, and *Spot the Dog*. When new children's books are adapted for films, TV series or computer games, sales of the books can increase still further and even the classics are given new life in this way.

The *Harry Potter* novels, movies, games and merchandise, for example, have made millions for the author, as well as for the original publisher and other publishers who produced translated editions in different languages throughout the world.

Significant profits can come from granting licences to other companies to produce and sell merchandise (anything from pencil cases to nightwear) associated with characters (even classic ones like Winnie the Pooh), so it is important to create a character (human or animal) that will appeal to children in a particular age range. This is a particular challenge for books that are targeted at younger children. Here the character must also be acceptable to the parent or grandparent who will buy the book and read it to (or with) the child. The influence of parents and grandparents in buying children's books is one reason why the books of authors such as Lewis Carroll, Beatrix Potter, Astrid Lindgren, C.S. Lewis and Antoine de Saint-Exupéry continue to sell with each new generation of children.

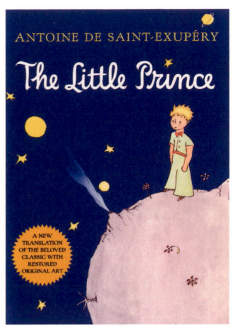

2.3

Audiobooks

Audiobooks were first produced in the 1930s as 'talking books' for people with blindness or other sight problems. They were usually available through specialist services or through schools and public libraries and they enjoyed some of the same tax and postal privileges as large print books.

Audiobooks have developed from the British Talking Books Service launched in 1935 with Agatha Christie's *The Murder of Roger Ackroyd* on 78 rpm shellac records; to the 1980s audiobooks produced in larger numbers for the commercial market on 33 rpm LP vinyl records, audio cassette and CD-ROM; to digital formats such as MP3.

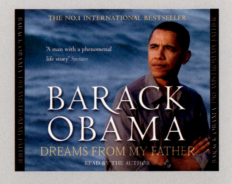

US sales of audiobooks were estimated at over $190 million in 2009 by the Audio Publishers Association; and in recent years Nielsen BookScan has estimated UK sales of audiobooks at over £20 million. *Dreams From My Father* is published by Canongate Books.

2.3
The Little Prince
The Little Prince, a childhood favourite for many, has a readership that crosses borders and generations. The novella, first published in 1943, is both the most read and most translated book in the French language, and was voted the best book of the twentieth century in France.

Words and pictures

The market for comic books, manga and BD *(bandes dessinées)* continues to grow. These formats are attractive to a broad range of readers of widely different ages, tastes and opinions. These, and the expanding range of graphic novels, are also adaptable to other media and can be used as the basis of animation, games, and a wide variety of digital and physical merchandise. *The Saga of Darren Shan* is published by HarperCollins.

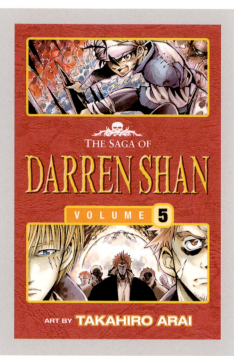

THE SAGA OF
DARREN SHAN
VOLUME **5**
ART BY **TAKAHIRO ARAI**

Other books for children and young adults (YA)

There are many types of books published for children, most obviously because children of different ages have varied interests, needs and reading abilities. Publishers are watching with great interest as a generation of true 'digital natives' grows up – the generation that has never known a world without mobile phones and the Internet. Now that very young children are familiar with the TV remote, the computer keyboard, and a broad array of mobile communications and games devices, it is possible that these will become the major ways today's young children will develop their 'reading habit'.

Whatever the channels for children's reading, some of the fundamental elements of publishing for the young are likely to remain. Authors and publishers must have a clear view of the age group and reading level of their target readers. The parents of many children may still want to expose them to a diet of more or less traditional stories.

Younger children – those who cannot yet read or who are just learning – are attracted by vivid engaging illustrations and simple, often repetitive, verbal patterns (whether in text or on audio).

Older age groups want to encounter strong narratives that bring to life the adventurous possibilities of the world, and show them how to withstand dangers and setbacks, while teenagers will surely always be rebellious and want to read about characters and plots that may worry their parents. This exploration of adolescent life, and the frequent coverage of personal issues that confront young people are at the basis of what publishers and booksellers call the young adult category. The broad popularity of some children's books like the *Harry Potter* series shows that adults are also attracted to some books originally written for children, and some types of children's publication have readers of all ages.

Working in trade and children's publishing

Editors working in trade fiction, non-fiction and children's publishing need a good feeling for nuances of language and a specific awareness of the language levels required for their target readers. When working with highly illustrated books that rely heavily on the relationship between words and images (many children's books and also books on subjects such as art, crafts and cooking), editors require a good understanding of how these elements support each other to deliver meaning to the reader.

As many trade and children's authors have literary agents, it is important to be a good negotiator and to have excellent personal communication skills. An international outlook and an awareness of other media trends are useful in exploiting the rights potential for adult trade and children's titles.

Educational publishing

Educational publishers produce books that are used in schools. They reflect the curriculum and educational structure of the market for which they are prepared, and are written for particular school levels. In the UK, where there is a national curriculum, educational publishing is mostly in the hands of a few large companies, and is divided according to the Four Key Stages (Primary 1 and 2, Secondary 3 and 4).

In the US, the 12 grades are divided into Elementary School (1–4), Middle School (5–8), and High School (9–12); the Kindergarten class (K) is usually included when talking of the entire educational system (K–12).

All countries have their own educational system, with different school years (for example, January to December, or October to June), trimesters, terms and semesters (two or three teaching periods per year), which determine the way in which educational publishing must develop material in order to deliver it at the appropriate time. Educational publishers need to understand the detailed requirements (and the procurement patterns) of the educational system in their country, state or province.

Educational publishers also produce a range of supplementary materials: teacher support packages (in print and online); testing and assessment materials; student handouts; dedicated websites; and audio and video materials. Increasingly, such product extensions (including textbooks, apps, study guides, classroom activities, calculating and charting exercises, interactive learning games and whiteboard exercises) are now available through digital channels. The structure of the both the physical and digital supply chain is centrally important to understanding the dynamics of the educational market.

In addition to understanding the mechanisms by which educational books, services and other materials are approved and purchased (centrally, by individual schools, or by parents), publishers also have to understand what educators prefer to receive in print and what they prefer to receive in digital forms.

The needs and expectations of educational customers are changing rapidly and publishers are making great investments to secure their market share. This makes it very difficult for new companies to enter the educational publishing market except in highly specialized niche areas.

Working in educational publishing
Editors in educational publishing usually have responsibility for a particular subject discipline at a specific level. So in the UK, he or she may be the Secondary Geography Editor, and in the US a title might be Editor of Elementary Math.

These editors often work with educational or curriculum advisors to ensure that their publications fit the needs of a particular school system, and they also work very closely with illustrators and designers to ensure that all elements of any published work combine to reinforce the educational objectives.

As multimedia packages are common in educational publishing, production coordinators need to have extensive knowledge of production in different media including audio and video.

The marketing and sales departments of educational publishers employ promotion and publicity managers to produce marketing literature and to develop social media and web communities. Sales representatives visit schools and education departments to promote the use of their company's products and services in individual schools and whole school systems. The goal of educational publishers is the adoption of a particular set of materials at either a school level or throughout an entire education system.

EFL/ELT Publishing

Over recent decades, the rise of English as the world language of business, education and popular culture has created a huge global market for English-language teaching and learning materials. This sector is variously known as EFL (English as a Foreign Language), ELT (English Language Teaching), or ESL (English as a Second Language) publishing. It is a highly competitive market, in which publishers such as Oxford University Press (OUP), Cambridge University Press (CUP) and Macmillan have been particularly successful. These firms invest heavily in keeping their brands at the forefront of the ELT market.

Language learning increasingly uses video, audio, digital practice and online assessment. Today's students often prefer digital reference materials (dictionaries and grammar guides) to traditional printed volumes. As learning English is now seen as a basic competence in many countries, local educational publishers are now much more active in producing textbooks and other teaching materials for their national markets.

Working in EFL publishing

EFL editors often have experience of teaching English, and tend to specialize in publishing for a particular region, such as Southern Europe, Asia or Latin America. They, and the sales force, work closely with language schools, teachers and other media companies in countries around the world, often in joint ventures with local publishing partners to develop materials and marketing networks.

Academic publishing

Academic publishing is closely related to the overall development of the tertiary (post-high school in the US) education sector; to trends in course development and delivery; national and international expenditure on the sector as a whole; and policies and funding that favour or disfavour specific areas of research and teaching. The audience for such publications is composed almost exclusively of people and institutions in the academic world, so there is a symbiotic relationship between the authors, publishers and readers of academic publications. Publishing of this type includes textbooks for university and college courses, supplementary readings, academic monographs and other publications produced by academics in the course of their research.

College and university textbooks

Some academic textbooks used in colleges and universities (such as Samuelson's *Economics* and Jansen's *History of Art*) are very successful. They sell in large quantities, year after year, and produce healthy profits for their authors and publishers. The texts are frequently updated and issued as new editions, and are published together with various product and service extensions (such as case studies, presentations, resource websites, and podcast lectures). They are expensive to develop and publishers spend a lot of time and resources to retain and increase market share in some highly competitive disciplines.

However, many academic books are not written or published in the hope of achieving vast sales, but each book seeks to fill a niche, even if this involves courses that have relatively small numbers of students.

For some years, many textbooks for degree level courses have been supplemented with online study and reference materials. Now that students are increasingly using e-readers to read and make notes on course textbooks, many texts are available as e-books. Just as consumer e-books have been adopted by the general reading public more rapidly in the US than elsewhere, so the use of e-textbooks has been greater in the US, where the NACS (National Association of College Stores) conducts regular surveys to monitor the increased use of e-texts. Recent research (such as the University of California Libraries Academic e-Book Usage Survey, 2011) indicates, however, that many students still prefer to use physical printed textbooks.

It is also common for publishers to offer university teaching staff the opportunity to produce texts customized for their particular course requirements. Using these services, university teachers can select content from a wide range of online material to be made up into a textbook specifically tailored to their needs. They can also add material of their own, or material from other sources that might have particular relevance to their course. The compilation is published on-demand, either as a short-run edition in the exact quantity required, as a POD book, or as an e-book. One example of such a custom textbook system is that offered by Wiley through their Wiley Custom Select service.

Monographs

Academic monographs (single subject book-length studies based on specialist research) were once a staple of academic and scholarly publishing. Such publications are now becoming less common, and PhD theses are no longer routinely transformed into book-length publications. Monographs have low sales (getting lower as academic library budgets decrease each year), and an academic monograph may not sell more than 100 copies. This means that prices for such printed books have become high, reducing sales still further in a vicious cycle of rising prices and diminishing sales, and leading to the e-publication of much monograph material.

The main reason academic writers want to publish academic monographs is to further their career, as publication is a necessary part of proving academic standing when looking for employment, promotion or tenure. As with essays and papers in academic journals, the extent to which such serious academic work is cited by other academics is sometimes seen as a measure of success for the publication, for the individual academics, and the institutions to which they belong.

Some academic monographs derive from PhD theses (dissertations) or from collections of papers presented at academic conferences. These special-interest publications, highly valuable to a select group of researchers, are migrating to e-publication, which is ideal for the purpose of dissemination to a small well-networked specialist group of readers, often spread throughout the world.

Monograph publications are also sometimes independently published by academic institutions or specialist centres. Those published by traditional publishers may be more likely to be distributed as part of a 'bundle' of such works sold on subscription to libraries and other institutional information services.

STM publishing

STM publishing (Scientific, Technical and Medical) is a major industry sector and includes textbooks, monographs, reference works, journals and other print and online services for the scientific, technical and medical communities. The value of the market for STM publications is much larger than that for academic publications in the humanities and social sciences. STM publishers are some of the biggest employers in the publishing industry, with a global turnover estimated at more than $20 billion (£12.6 billion) (International Association of Scientific, Technical and Medical Publishers).

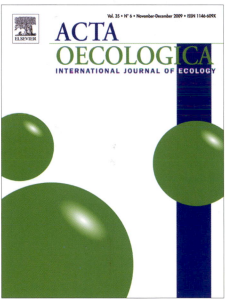

2.4

**2.4
ACTA Oecologica
and The American
Journal of Pathology**
STM journals are used by researchers throughout the world to disseminate the results of their work, and career success can depend on publication in the most prestigious journals. These journals are published by Elsevier.

Sales and marketing

Sales and marketing in STM publishing uses the analysis of citations, trends and other metrics. You can learn more about this complex area from the website of the International Association of Scientific, Technical and Medical Publishers and the Association of Learned and Professional Society Publishers (ALPSP).

While the large commercial publishers, university presses and professional organizations (such as the Institute of Physics and the American Chemical Society) dominate this sector, there are many other smaller academic and scholarly publishing operations working across the academic spectrum. These smaller outfits often have close working relationships with the major companies who produce and market the publications, while the organization retains editorial control.

Working in academic and STM publishing

In the academic and STM sector, product managers, senior editors, and publishing editors manage publications in a particular subject area, producing journals, monographs, digital resources, and even workshops, seminars and conferences. They spend time networking with people involved in their special discipline, and work closely with external journal editors, series editors and other editorial advisors drawn from academic departments and research institutes.

It is common for these editors and managers to have a background in the relevant specialism, particularly for very technical subjects such as engineering or medicine.

Given the importance of digital workflow to STM and scholarly publishing, the person in charge is sometimes called a production editor, and this person is also likely to have a significant input into marketing, working with exhibitions managers and promotion executives. As digital publishing is the mainstream activity for most STM publishers, the idea of having a specific information system manager is declining and everyone is expected to work with digital publishing (although the physical production and distribution of books and journals is still important in some subjects).

Reference publishing

Reference publishing has some crossover with academic publishing as well as providing reference materials for a wide variety of professions, such as law and accountancy. Reference publishers produce resources such as encyclopædias, dictionaries and directories.

This was one of the first sectors in publishing to take advantage of digital technologies, as very large quantities of data can be gathered, manipulated, stored, updated and distributed far more effectively in this way than by traditional print methods.

Reference publishing has also been affected by the growth of Wikipedia. This free, online reference website was founded in 2001 and has around four million articles in English and versions in 283 languages making a total of over 20 million articles, nearly two million images and over 30 million active users. It is put together on a volunteer basis by thousands of experts and users throughout the world. Wikipedia has radically altered the market for encyclopædias most notably that of the previous market leader, *Encyclopædia Britannica*, which in 2012 announced that it was ceasing publication of the 32-volume printed edition.

Trade reference books

Some reference books, like *Guinness World Records*, are really trade books (hence the label trade reference books). The *Guinness World Records* brand is an example of the kind of trade reference publishing that has been developed in recent years to include a wide variety of media manifestations including websites, video, games, and interactive media. Travel reference brands like *Lonely Planet* and *Rough Guides* are other examples of trade reference publishing that have moved to digital platforms.

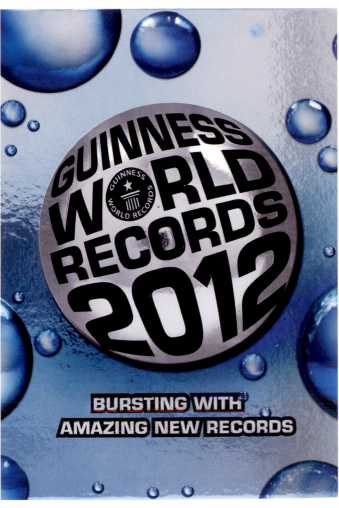

2.5

2.5
Guinness World Records
Since the first edition in 1955, *The Guinness Book of Records* has been a popular gift book and is a classic example of trade reference publishing. This annual publication (renamed *Guinness World Records*) provides a wealth of fascinating information and encourages people to strive to beat a range of world records.

Discussion questions

1. What are the differences between the authors of trade books and academic books?

2. What are the differences between working in educational publishing and STM publishing?

3. Which types of publishing were the first to adopt digital publishing formats?

4. Are the differences between different types of publishing becoming less or more important?

Print, e-books, m-books and iBooks

The rapid growth of e-book publishing in the recent past sometimes makes it hard to remember and appreciate the radical changes to publishing that this has brought about, but it is also important to understand which basic elements of publishing have changed and which have remained the same.

2.6

```
<?xml version="1.0"?>
<quiz>
 <question>
 Who was the forty-second
 president of the U.S.A.?
 </question>
 <answer>
 William Jefferson Clinton
 </answer>
 <!-- Note: We need to add
 more questions later.-->
</quiz>
```

XML

2.6
XML markup
This piece of text has been marked up using XML. The style for <quiz>, <question> or <answer> can be specified at a later date depending on the format of the finished print or digital publication.

Production systems

Production systems are likely to remain flexible in publishing and, through the use of XML or other ways of creating and adapting content, publishers continue to be free to decide to produce publications in print or in digital formats from the same content files. The tools are becoming more sophisticated as new platforms are developed, and the way in which publishers turn an author's work into a published product continue to evolve. We will look at book design and production in more detail in Chapter 5, but the fundamental aspect to remember at this stage is that any design and production system must be adaptable to both current and new methods of production and distribution, whatever form of print or digital publication the ever-changing technology may make possible.

Origins and future of e-books

Electronic books have a longer history than you might think. Project Gutenberg, the oldest digital library of electronic texts, was started in 1971 in the very early days of the Internet and now offers over 38,000 free e-books. Franklin Electronic Publishers launched the first commercially available hand-held reader in 1986. Following the success of the Spelling Ace electronic spelling corrector, Franklin has produced many other titles including dictionaries, medical reference works, and an extensive range of Franklin Electronic Bibles.

Much of the development of electronic publications, mostly accessible through large computer networks, was originally focused on publications for the research, reference and educational markets. Many of the systems used to access research publications today date back to those early days of electronic publication on academic networks.

Several e-readers had limited success around the turn of the century, including the SoftBook (launched 1998), the Rocket e-book (2000) and the Microsoft Reader (launched 2000 and due for phase-out in August 2012).

After the US launch of the Kindle in 2007, the e-reader started to become a mass consumer item and the e-book's challenge to printed books became a reality in the market place. These changes continue and it is likely to be some years until the publishing market re-enters a period of relative stability. As with many technological developments, the development of e-books has seen a proliferation of different systems for the production of e-books and the devices on which they can be read, and innovations in display that have come with the development of backlit screens and e-ink.

At the hardware end, the Sony e-book reader, Kindle and Nook are just some of the devices that have been developed. The Amazon Kindle and the Apple iPad, in particular, have been influential in driving the development of the e-book market sector, using new business models such as the 'agency' model (see page 36).

There has also been competition between the different software used to produce e-book files, although common standards are beginning to be adopted by most publishers and device manufacturers. The development of diverse hardware and software has reflected the different aspirations of global media companies as varied as Amazon and Apple, Sony and News International. Various legal battles concerning patents and proprietary software have been a feature of the jostling for market position.

As the industry matures, there are concerted industry moves to establish standards that would apply over different platforms and publication types. EPUB®, a standard distribution format, developed by the International Digital Publishing Forum, is intended to enable the interoperability of digital books and other digital publications between different reading devices and applications, and you will find more about this in Chapter 6.

2.7
Kindle Fire
Kindle has developed from being a medium for text-only e-books, to a platform for illustrated books, magazines, children's books and other media. The functions of the e-reader and multi-purpose tablet are blending together as the market develops and consumers become more familiar with the use of such devices.

2.7

Are e-books just another format?

When it became clear that e-books were here to stay, publishers needed to start looking at the new formats that e-publishing offered. It's worth looking at how some of these new formats affect readers.

◉ You need special equipment to read an e-book. But this equipment may be something you can use for other entertainment and communication purposes. The company selling the e-books often has access to the customer's device, so is able to target future promotions on the basis of a customer profile created from information gathered.

◉ You usually buy an e-book online (although some traditional booksellers are now offering e-books for sale), and it will either be downloaded to your device and/ or stored in a far-off server – in the 'cloud'.

◉ Browsing an e-book shop is different because e-books do not have physical covers or standard-length blurbs. The 'shop window' of an e-bookshop can provide a wealth of information, including things like author interviews, reader reviews and 'look inside' functions.

◉ Graphics are used heavily in e-book sales and promotion, and blurbs have developed into extensive (often multimedia) promotional messages circulated via social networks, viral marketing tools and dedicated websites.

◉ Length, page size and, increasingly, typography, are no longer a barrier to either publisher or reader. Short books like Kindle Singles have proliferated as e-books. Page sizes and design features are determined by the capabilities of the software and hardware, not by the practicalities and economics of physical production. Readers of e-books may be able to choose type size, typeface and page layout. Audiobook publishers may increasingly offer a range of voices that will read the book out loud from the digital file.

◉ It is possible to borrow an e-book from a library but more difficult to borrow one from a friend.

◉ Self-publishing is much more viable with e-books, although it isn't usually as easy as it looks!

◉ The e-book is not just another format to be added to the hardback, trade paperback and mass-market paperback. The pricing strategies that were used to exploit different sectors of the market for physical books are over time no longer workable. It is also possible to produce enhanced e-books, with embedded videos, pop-up graphics and animation.

In the life of a typical trade title, the original launch in hardback would be followed after some months by the publication of a large 'B' format 'trade' paperback edition (see page 126), and eventually, if sales warranted, a mass-market paperback. This consecutive publishing model has now been disrupted, and the hardback edition (marketable at a higher price) has become a standard format for what publishers hope will be bestselling trade books – fiction and non-fiction – particularly in the US.

However, the previous ordered progression from one format to the next, as markets were progressively exploited with different distribution and pricing, has been superseded by a simultaneous publication of p-book and e-book, usually in different formats of both. In a similar and parallel development first seen in Asia, mobile technology has led to the development of books designed to be read on mobile telephones (m-books known as *keitai shosetsu* in Japan), and these ultra-short books are mirrored in some of the publications now being published for tablets and games devices.

The application called iBooks was developed by Apple; it enables the user of an iPad to download and read e-books. iBooks includes the iBookstore, and offers the facility to keep a personal collection of iBooks on the iCloud, so that they can be viewed on the iPad, iPhone or iPod touch.

'I think publishers have been very focused on how to replicate the book in digital form, and very focused on the novel. But is that the right format? How does that fit into the world of gaming and social media where there are so many calls on the consumer's time? Is it necessarily about 80,000 words now?'

Jonathan Williams, BoxFiction, 2011

E-book covers

Can you tell an e-book by looking at its cover? It doesn't physically have one, but, in spite of video and audio promotions for e-books, readers still like to have a static 'image', something that looks like the traditional cover of a hardback or paperback book. Without such an image, the job of the marketer becomes much more difficult.

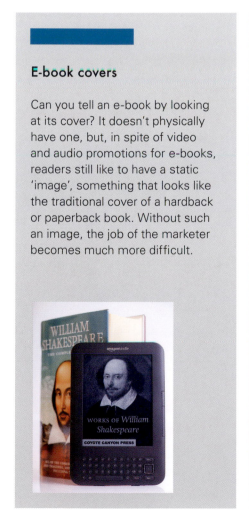

Discussion questions

1. What do you think are some of the most important digital innovations of the past 30 years, 10 years, and 12 months?

2. How have these innovations changed the reader's perception of the 'book'?

3. How can readers customize e-books and other digital publications?

4. What are some of the major differences between p-books and e-books?

Journals, magazines and newspapers

While book publishing is our primary concern, it cannot be seen in complete isolation from other long-established parts of the larger publishing industry with which it has a close and symbiotic relationship. Other forms of publishing, such as magazines and newspapers, are also an established part of the global publishing environment and it's worth considering some of the ways in which the book publishing ecology is developing in relation to these types of publishing.

Journals

Journal publishing was one of the first sectors to adopt digital publication and distribution. The new production and distribution models were ideal for managing a wide variety of content from many different sources, and for packaging and distributing this to a dispersed international readership easily. While there are still some journals that are available only in paper formats, many are published in both p- and e-versions, or exclusively as e-journals.

Journal are most commonly used in university and research institutions, and 'packages' can be purchased from suppliers such as EBSCO (see the case study on page 65) giving access to vast numbers of current and back issues of journals. The economies of digital production and distribution mean that even the smallest organizations now find it cost-effective to produce regular publications.

STM journals are the primary way in which research is evaluated, validated and disseminated. Scholarly communications in the humanities and social sciences, are also an essential part of the development and exchange of ideas. Many STM and scholarly journals are based around the membership of particular societies or special networks of people interested in an area of intellectual enquiry.

Journal publishing is dominated by a small number of international publishers (such as Elsevier, Springer and Wiley) and is one area of publishing that has been most active in asserting the central importance of intellectual property ownership rights, DRM (digital rights management, see page 155) and DOI standards in the face of open access and fair use movements.

DOI

The Digital Object Identifier (DOI®) System is a way of identifying specific units of content, such as an electronic document. DOI names are assigned to any entity for use on digital networks. This name does not change even if the object to which it refers is moved to another server or owner. Using DOI names as identifiers is intended to make it easier to manage intellectual property and the income that may be derived from it.

2.8
Saga Magazine
The target readers of *Saga Magazine* would instantly recognize the actress Sheila Hancock, a baby boomer icon. Advertising in magazines like this reaches the over-50 age group, which Saga says has 'a collective pot of £175 billion of disposable income', which is greater than any other age group.

2.8

Magazines

In spite of the need to adapt to digital publishing, print magazines have continued to prosper and many new magazines have been launched in the twenty-first century. Magazines make their money through newsstand sales, subscriptions and advertising revenues. Most consumer magazines rely heavily on the regular publication of a print version, often publishing different language and territory editions under a common brand name (*Elle* magazine, for example, has 43 different international editions). Some consumer magazines (often those dealing with celebrities and media gossip) retain a mass appeal and sell through newsstands at a low cover price in large quantities.

The pattern of consumer magazine distribution varies in different countries, with, for example, the US market being traditionally more reliant on regular subscriptions than the market in the UK. With a business model heavily based on advertising revenues, UK consumer magazines tend to have an online offer that mirrors and complements the advertising audience of the print version.

As portable e-readers become more able to reproduce the vibrant colour illustrations and complex layouts that we are used to seeing in consumer magazines, this market sector is moving to include other digital formats and is increasing its output of video, audio and other dynamic content, for example Elle TV.

Special interest magazines
Special interest magazines (covering anything from photography to computers, gardening to travel, antiques to automobiles) can often have quite large circulations. Some command high cover and subscription prices and remain successful in attracting advertisers to their print versions and websites, as they are major communication channels to niche markets for specialist goods and services.

One area of circulation growth is magazines for the now ageing 'baby boomers': *AARP Magazine* (over 20 million subscribers) in the US and *Saga Magazine* in the UK (over 600,000 subscribers and nearly 1.5 million readers over the age of 50 each month) are among the highest circulation magazines — an indication of a growing market that is of importance to publishers and advertisers.

'… we strove to replicate the look and the feel of the magazine, using the same typefaces and developing a design that was comfortable to read. That being said, we did want to make use of the technology. We decided we would use these iPad extras sparingly and quietly. Word is still king . . .'

Pamela Maffei McCarthy, deputy editor of The New Yorker, *2011*

2.9
The Bookseller
The Bookseller has been the leading UK business magazine for the book industry since 1858. The website provides daily news and comment about the book business, with regular news updates throughout the day.

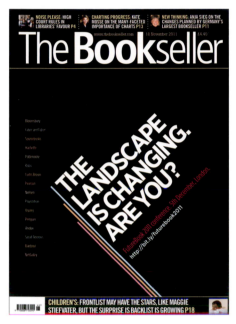

2.9

Trade magazines

Trade magazines represent another specialized media sector, produced for people who work in a specific industry. *The Bookseller*, *Publishers Weekly*, *Printing News*, and *American Printer* (all available online) are examples of trade magazines for the publishing industry. Trade magazines in the publishing world span both p- and e-formats and they are still adapting to the changing reading habits and information requirements of people working in the sector. Those industries that are most involved in the move to a digital information environment are, by and large, the ones where e-publication has mostly taken over from print trade magazines, and this seems to be the case with the trade press that relates to the publishing industry.

Many trade magazines have what is known as a 'controlled circulation', meaning that free subscriptions are sent to members of a target market that belong to a particular trade or profession: a valuable target group for specialist advertisers. This is in contrast to the paid circulation recorded in the case of consumer magazines.

Newspapers

The newspaper industry has undergone rapid change in the digital environment, suffering a decline of advertising revenues, competition from free news services in other media and online, the growth of social networking and citizen journalism, and the extension of digital communication into all aspects of public and private life. Newspapers are experimenting with a variety of digital business models including various types of subscription schemes, pay-per-use systems, and targeting advertising based on customer profiles.

The connections between press media and the publishing of books, journals and magazines are historically rich and diverse. For example, HarperCollins, which publishes both p- and e-books, is owned by News Corporation which also publishes newspapers such as the *Wall Street Journal* and *The Sunday Times*.

Discussion questions

1. In addition to Amazon, Apple and Google, which non-publishing companies have become important to publishing since 2000?

2. Which models from other digital media (music, movies, games) might be applied to publishing in future?

3. Which e-readers existed before the Kindle?

4. What is STM publishing and how is it different from other forms of book publishing?

Journals, magazines and newspapers

Chapter 2: The choices publishers make
Who will pay, and how?

Who will pay, and how?

Everyone in publishing is involved in one way or another in the 'value chain'. At each stage, value is added by the performance of a specific function, an action or transaction. This added value is eventually realized when there is a transaction in which the goods or services satisfy the requirements of the end-user.

How do publishers make money?

All businesses require a favourable balancing of their income and expenditure. In the case of publishers, they need to generate a surplus to continue to acquire, develop, produce and distribute their publications. They keep track of their income and expenditure by the 'profit and loss' (or P & L) account. If you are serious about a career in publishing, you must never think that finance is 'someone else's job', so don't think of skipping over those sections in this book that cover finance!

The levels of investments are different in different types of publishing. Educational publishing may require a high level of research, testing, and compliance with curriculum requirements and educational quality assurance (QA) standards. The same will be true for publishers of teaching materials for major courses in higher levels of education and this must be taken into account when planning budgets for this kind of publication. Similarly, reference publications must be planned to incorporate the financial costs of collecting, organizing and updating data on a regular, if not continuous, basis.

The design and production costs of publishing trade and children's books will vary greatly, but perception of quality remains equally important to buyers of p-books and to readers looking for enhanced user experience from e-books.

Even if some of the costs of physical reproduction, mass production and stock (inventory) holding are reducing in the digital world, costs associated with product development, design, marketing and operability may well increase as publishers strive to satisfy the enhanced expectations of the market.

The publishing value chain

All of the value added by the author, publisher and distributor must be recouped from the eventual sale to the consumer.

Market research and editorial plan (content development)

Financing and publishing decisions (investment and risk management)

Product development and production (quality control – process management)

Marketing, sales and distribution (channel control)

Marketing and customer satisfaction (market communication)

Journals, magazines and newspapers

Chapter 2: The choices publishers make
Who will pay, and how?

What income?

Each sale of a printed book generates an income for the publisher related to the price the customer pays. For example, a book priced at £10.00 (or $/€10.00), if sold at full price, means that a customer will pay £10.00 (or $/€10.00) for the book, or maybe less if the bookseller is selling the book at a discount or on a special offer.

If the book is bought from a bookseller, he or she pockets the sales income (10.00 or less) and pays the publisher a price calculated with a percentage discount from the publisher's price (usually between 45 to 50 per cent, but anywhere up to 70 per cent in the case of supermarkets and e-booksellers). So the publisher's net income (Net Sales Revenue – NSR) is usually between 30–55 per cent of a book's list price. With this, the publisher has to pay for the costs of developing and producing the book, paying the author, promoting the book, paying the other overhead expenses of the business (salaries, office costs, utilities) and hopefully producing some profit.

In addition to revenue from sales, some publishers receive additional income from the subsidiary rights (such as translation, adaptation and serialization rights). These may be included in the publisher-author contract with income being split between them on an agreed percentage basis.

In trade publishing many subsidiary rights (paperback, translation, film and other adaptation rights) now tend to be handled directly by the author's agent.

Book publishers are now developing new sources of revenue, for example:

- Textbook e-book rental schemes
- Advertising
- 'Slice and dice' usage tracked by Digital Object Identifiers or watermarks
- Time-sensitive access
- Pay walls
- Individual and bundled subscriptions

How a publisher may get 10% profit!		
Publisher's cover price	10.00	
Bookseller's price (promotional price to customer)		7.99
Bookseller pays publisher cover price less 45%	5.50	
Publishers net income (net sales revenue – NSR)	5.50	
Less		
Author's royalty (10% of NSR)		0.55
Production cost (approx. 20% of NSR)		1.10
Marketing, warehouse, distribution and unsold stock costs (approx. 30% of NSR)		1.65
Other overhead costs (i.e. salaries, office costs, insurance, etc.) (30% of NSR)		1.65
Publisher's profit 5.50 – 0.55 – 1.10 – 1.65 – 1.65	0.55 (10% of NSR)	

Discussion questions

1. What is the most important thing to take into account when deciding to publish a book?

2. Why do different types of publishing need to take the level of investment into account?

3. How do publishers 'add value'?

4. What is Net Sales Revenue?

Case study:

Amazon and

EBSCO

A number of large enterprises have recently emerged in publishing distribution, and this case study looks at two of these: Amazon (a name that is probably familiar) and EBSCO (which may not be).

Amazon

Amazon is one of the biggest and most recognizable brands in the world. The company works ceaselessly to consolidate its position as a major supplier of many kinds of consumer goods, including publications. Through its book supply system it has a commanding market share of the supply of printed books, and by the launch of consecutive versions of the Kindle, it has been one of the most important companies in the development of the market sector for e-books.

- The Amazon online bookstore opened in 1995, stocking and selling physical books, first in the US, and rapidly expanding to the UK, Europe and Asia. When books started to be produced by print-on-demand, Amazon quickly linked their supply systems with a major POD supplier, and then came Amazon Kindle.

- By monitoring their online behaviour, Amazon profiles its customers in order to target promotions via email and during visits to the website. Amazon encourages users to write reviews and make recommendations. This adds to the information it holds on visitors to the site, and information that it gathers through the analysis of customer browsing patterns.

- The Amazon website is user friendly, and through effective SEO (search engine optimization) Amazon ranks highly on searches for an author or book title.

2.10

2.10
Kindle
Amazon has continually adapted and innovated to build, and now maintain, its market share. Its Kindle e-reader has put it at the forefront of e-book adoption by the mass consumer market.

- Amazon is now becoming a significant publisher in its own right, particularly in genres such as romance, mystery and westerns. It has also developed self-publishing packages for the Kindle.

- Amazon is an international company with websites aimed at many major markets (Amazon.com, amazon.co.uk, amazon.de, and amazon.cn). By 2012 it had over 50 distribution centres in North America, Europe and Asia.

EBSCO

EBSCO was established in 1944 and now bills itself as 'the world's leading information agent'.

- EBSCO subscription services are used by tens of thousands of institutions worldwide, representing millions of end-users.

- EBSCO services enable information creators and users to manage content, including print and e-journals, e-packages, research databases, and e-books. Its services are used by university and research libraries to manage their collections and to provide integrated services to researchers and other library users.

- EBSCO provides support services to its users to ensure that software is compatible, language needs are met, and training is given to librarians and users.

- EBSCO supplies e-books and audiobooks to libraries in three different ways: an ownership model based on the number of users that can access an e-book at any given time; a subscription model that offers large collections of titles in high-interest subject areas; and a lease model under which e-books can be made available through a library system for a limited period.

- EBSCO is committed to energy conservation and other green measures, and also provides free universal access to GreenFILE, a research database focusing on the relationship between human beings and the environment. GreeenFILE covers information on topics ranging from global warming to recycling to alternative fuel sources, and contains scholarly and general interest titles, as well as government documents and reports.

Key points

Amazon and EBSCO have developed supply-chain businesses that control supply to a large part of their respective markets. This gives them great influence with the following results.

◉ **Publishers** now develop their products and services with specific attention paid to the needs of these channels.

◉ **Customers** increasingly have little choice but to deal with them.

◉ **The financial terms** of the relationship between publishers and the supply chain (discounts and/or commissions) are to some extent dictated by these companies.

◉ **Other companies**, such as independent booksellers and library suppliers, find it hard to compete and often go out of business, particularly in countries where there is no legal or customary fixed price regime for publications.

◉ **Global distribution** of e-books and other digital publications has made it easier for these companies to conduct business successfully on an international basis. Issues of freight, customs and taxation are more easily reconciled for intangible products than they are for physical publications.

◉ **Territorial rights** are a major concern of these supply-chain giants. Their interests are advanced if global territorial market rights are established.

◉ **Library usage** of publications supplied by these companies (and use by non-authorized readers) is increasingly controlled by both specific license agreements and security software.

◉ **Sustainability and environment responsibility** are important to some companies connected with publishing. The use of energy by the industry is a matter of concern for some, as firms such as Amazon and EBSCO utilize large server farms to store data and as a result, large amounts of energy are expended in operating and keeping cool the servers.

Activity

Larger companies are increasingly dominating the distribution of all types of publication, from bestselling trade books, to STM and scholarly journals, and self-published POD (print on demand) and e-books. Some groups of smaller publishers, such as the Faber and Faber Independent Alliance, and groups of independent booksellers such as the American Booksellers Association Indie Bound, have come together to act as a counterpoint to them.

1. What can smaller distribution outlets offer to make them competitive in the market?

2. Is it possible for smaller firms to develop e-book distribution systems that are attractive to consumers?

3. Can book buyers be persuaded to pay higher prices for a more personal service?

4. Can you identify any similar schemes which encourage smaller publishing companies to develop alternative supply chains?

5. Can you identify other publishing-related companies that have shown a concrete commitment to the environment, similar to ESBCO's GreenFILE?

Chapter 3

Writers, readers and intermediaries

Publishers connect readers with writers, and they do this by working with other people who have specialist skills. The people involved in this process of communication and dissemination are sometimes envisaged as a 'book chain', which contains several distinct groups, such as writers, publishers, printers, booksellers, libraries, and readers: all linked together in a linear way to convey a message from the creator to the user of a published text. All the component links of this 'book chain' are seen as necessary to ensure the smooth functioning of the process.

This consecutive linear process – from author to editor to designer to production to sales, marketing and distribution – has developed into a more complex network, in which members work in a far more inter-related and interdependent way.

It is now even more important to understand the roles of the different intermediaries and how they interact, and while subsequent chapters will look at the editorial (Chapter 4), design and production (Chapter 5), and marketing (Chapter 7) functions, this chapter particularly focuses on how the author's role in the 'book chain' or 'book network' is affected by the various intermediaries.

Authors, illustrators, creators and their rights

From the point at which an author first envisages preparing a work for publication, he or she becomes involved in communicating with others about it. The first significant milestone in this communication is often the preparation of a publishing proposal.

Book proposal

The relationship between author and publisher usually begins with the publishing proposal, a document that lays out the rationale for a particular book.

Proposals for fiction might include a plot outline and details of the major characters and setting. Non-fiction proposals typically identify a working title and give a brief description of the work. This proposal will include a synopsis of the book; the reasons why the title is needed by the marketplace; its intended level and approach to the subject; and a list of the key features. In most cases the author also provides a detailed outline of the book, its proposed structure and chapter headings; and the estimated length of the work. The publisher will want to know the author's views on primary and secondary markets for the proposed title, with key selling features and details of any competition. Details of the author's experience and professional standing, and the titles (and sales history) of any previous publications will also be useful in evaluating the proposal.

What's all this about 'content'?

On the basis of the publishing proposal, authors and publishers both hope to get some financial reward from the creation and publication of the work, which will entail developing specific content. By using the term 'content', publishers and other media industries denote the intangible intellectual property (IP), that can be 'owned', 'controlled', 'exploited', 'managed', 'versioned', and 'delivered' to customers, consumers, and other users in various formats and on different digital platforms.

Content can be seen in terms of being 'a bundle of rights' (not only the rights to produce a book-length publication, but also a variety of subsidiary rights). Everyone with an interest in these rights (authors, agents, publishers and other media companies) will seek to protect their entitlement to benefit from them.

Content management in the digital media environment is a complex task, and each day brings new challenges as original work is adapted for an array of media, such as games, apps and animations. It requires skills in editorial development, design, and physical and digital production to do this. Because of these complexities, publishers have extended their networks of collaboration to encompass skills from a broad range of IT professionals, game designers, brand architects and digital innovators.

The value of the content of any work is thus a combination of the intrinsic value that results from the originality and expertise used to create a work; and the skill and sensitivity with which the material is adapted to appeal to a particular readership. Important, too, is the effective communication of the potential value of the work to an audience that may gain access to it through a variety of means: purchase, official loan, unofficial borrowing, sharing, communities, and even illegal copying. Both formal and informal networks play a part in this process.

3.1
The Cat in the Hat
Dr. Seuss created
The Cat in the Hat
specifically to
support literacy
learning in the US.
The book, published
by HarperCollins,
uses a restricted
vocabulary of simple
words. The rhythms
and rhymes make
this a perfect book for
the learning reader.

3.1

Authorship

Until recently, many writers and
illustrators were resistant to adopting
non-bookish methods of communication
and distribution, and some authors
still think of the book primarily in
its physical printed manifestation,
while accepting and even welcoming
the possibility of publication in e-book
formats. Authors generally identify
themselves as working in a particular
genre or type of publishing (for example
literary fiction, or guidebooks) but
there is now a tendency for successful
authors to extend their writing into
new, often more lucrative, areas (such
as cookery books or autobiography).
Some illustrators, photographers and
graphic artists, and a small but
growing number of avant-garde
authors, are at the forefront of
exploring new models such as non-
consecutive text, multiple narratives
and readers' contributions. Most of
this experimental publishing is done
by smaller publishers or by the
writers and artists themselves.

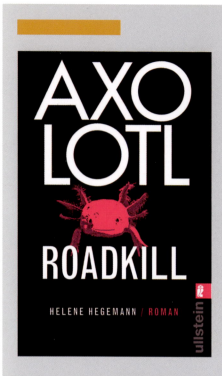

New views of authenticity and ownership

Authorship implies (and in the case of the author's contractual relationship with a publisher, it requires a guarantee of) originality, but even this is under question in the digital publishing environment. In 2010 Helene Hegemann's controversial novel *Axolotl Roadkill*, published by Ullstein, showed that some authors now see writing as being akin to the musical remix or software 'mashup', in which other people's writing is adapted without acknowledgement or permission. Hegemann maintains that what she called authenticity rather than originality is now the important thing about writing – you can, she maintains, use other authors' works so long as you arrange it in an original way.

In another example, Michel Houellebecq used some Wikipedia entries (including a description of how flies have sex) for his 2010 novel *La Carte et le Térritoire* without acknowledgement. If anyone can edit these words, the argument runs, why cannot anyone use them?

The sometimes unclear status of works published on the Internet, and the belief that not everything has to be subject to a strict regime of intellectual property (IP) ownership, has been accompanied by the development of Creative Commons licences, which 'provide a free, public, and standardized infrastructure that creates a balance between the reality of the Internet and the reality of copyright laws'.

The standardized Creative Commons licences do not replace copyright, although they are based on it. They allow different kinds of re-use where no commercial compensation is sought by the copyright owner.

The craft of writing

Authorship, as recognized by publishers, reviewers and readers, represents the exercise of a skill in communicating with an audience. A central part of the publishing process is the way in which agents and editors work with authors to develop their writing abilities; consolidate their awareness of how best to communicate with their readership; and provide a framework that nurtures successful authorship, effective publishing and satisfied readers. The process of working with a professional agent or editor is a major way in which writers have traditionally learnt their craft.

3.2
Kazuo Ishiguro
Kazuo Ishiguro, prize-winning author of *Never Let Me Go* and *Remains of the Day*, studied Creative Writing at the University of East Anglia in the UK, on the postgraduate course established by Malcolm Bradbury. Bradbury once said that when he proposed starting the course 'it was then generally believed in Britain that creative writing was a dangerous American import, like the McDonald Hamburger, and no-one would ever eat it.' (Photo by Jane Bown)

3.2

These days there is a healthy debate about whether good writing can be taught, and many MA and MFA courses cover the craft of writing: from scientific and technical writing, to travel and food writing, to poetry and the amorphous field known as creative writing. These courses attempt to systematize the learning of authorship skills, and have been commercially successful for some. Many prominent literary authors have attended such courses, including Ian McEwan, Kazuo Ishiguro, Anne Enright, and Tracy Chevalier, who have all emerged from the University of East Anglia Creative Writing Course in the UK since 1970.

In the US there are MFA courses at over 300 universities, such as those at NYU, University of Texas at Austin, and University of California at Irvine.

Author's rights

Authors, illustrators and anyone else who creates something that may be published, all have rights in what they have created, whether it is published or not. While an idea (or indeed a book title) is not protected by copyright law, the moment the idea is expressed (written down, sketched or noted on an electronic device) it becomes the intellectual property of the creator and may not be used by anyone else without his or her agreement. As we have already seen in Chapter 1, these rights are protected by copyright laws enacted by the legislative bodies in most countries of the world, and are given international recognition through the Berne Convention.

Creators grant a licence to publishers to exploit the rights that they have in their work in many different ways. The usual method of payment is by a percentage royalty on the publisher's income. At the time of contract (or on publication) an advance may be paid against anticipated future royalties. On many occasions work done by an author is considered 'work for hire' and the ownership rests with the person who has paid the author's fee, usually the publisher. Chapter 4 explores the way in which the negotiation of the contract fits into the editorial process.

Intellectual Property Management (IPM) is one of the fundamentals of commercial publishing. Without it, those who create content and who determine how the content is presented to readers (the 'arrangement') could not assert their legal right to benefit from its production and distribution. The digital culture has led publishers and authors to fear a rapid increase in unauthorized copying and file sharing (otherwise known as piracy) similar to that experienced for recorded music, film and computer games. Developments in digital rights management have created complex structures to map and manage all sorts of content, from book-length publications to very short copyright elements, sometimes referred to as 'granular' content.

Discussion questions

1. What might be included in a publishing proposal?

2. Is digital publishing changing our views of what constitutes original publishing content?

3. Can authorship be learned?

4. Why is copyright important? Is adapting and incorporating someone else's work without acknowledgement becoming more acceptable? Do you see plagiarism becoming more or less important in the future of publishing?

Agents and other gatekeepers

Although they now represent the interests of authors across the publishing landscape, literary agents play a more important role in trade and children's publishing, to the extent that it is now very difficult to get published by many established trade publishing houses without the intercession of an agent. Gone are the days when a publisher's reader would wade through the 'slush pile' of unsolicited manuscripts.

Even when works that have not been commissioned or not come to the publisher via an agent are financially successful, the authors are then often signed up by an agent. Although this may mean that publishers have to pay more, such arrangements are often to the advantage of the author, the publisher, and – of course – the agent.

The author's relationship with publishers and agents

The editor is often a very important person in developing an author's style and career, working with the author on the book proposal and on the work in progress; preparing manuscripts for publication; and acting as a friend and mentor throughout the author's career. To some extent, though, the editor's role has diminished in this century and been replaced by that of the author's agent, in particular for authors writing fiction.

Agents seek to identify promising talent at an early stage, develop a publishing strategy, and negotiate the best deal on behalf of the author with publishers and other media outlets at home and abroad. A good agent will get more income for the author, add value to the author's brand, and help to develop a credible media platform from which other activities can be pursued. Agents typically receive a percentage of the payments that they negotiate for an author's work, usually around 15 per cent on home sales, and 20 per cent on transatlantic and most other rights. There are specialist agents who handle big money negotiations such as film rights.

The author's agent may now take on some of the editor's responsibilities, such as providing editorial guidance and approving the final copy, influencing promotion and publicity campaigns, and developing other income possibilities. These may include personal appearances, product endorsements, and lucrative media spin-offs, for example in TV and radio.

Since the post-2010 explosion of the e-book as a format for the general reading public, some agents (such as Andrew Wylie and Ed Victor) have launched e-book services of their own. These agent-led e-book publishing activities were intended to benefit authors who receive a much bigger share of the income (50%) than they would from traditional publishing deals.

Royalties, fees and agents

A publisher pays the author a royalty on sales according to a schedule agreed in the contract.
While the range of royalties will vary, they will tend to be in the following ranges.

Royalty payments	
Hardback	In the range of 5–12% (of cover price) or 10–15% (of net sales receipts – NSR)
Trade paperback	Usually less than the hardback royalty rate (in a range 5–10% of NSR)
E-book	Growing from a base of 15–25% to 40–50% of digital net receipts
Translation rights	50% of publisher's receipts (what is received from the publisher of the foreign language edition)
Other subsidiary rights	40–60% of publisher's receipts

Other potentially high-value rights, such as film and merchandizing rights, are subject to negotiation.

The way in which agents are now acting as publishers for their clients is another
indication that the traditional linear functions implied by the book chain are taking
on a new form in the current network environment.

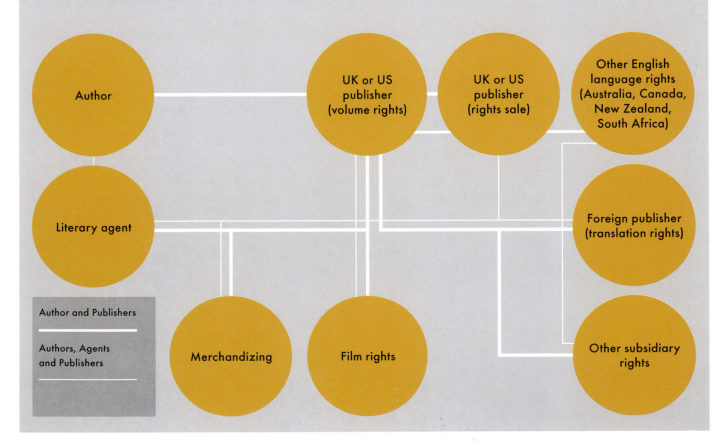

The publisher's relationship with agents

Publishers recognize that dealing with agents can make their life easier. Negotiations with agents may be tougher than they used to be with financially naïve authors, but the two sides are, in general, speaking the same language. Every clause of the author-publisher contract doesn't need to be explained afresh to each new author. Payments are made and reconciled with a smaller number of fellow professionals, and can be discussed in terms that all parties understand.

On the other hand, agents may hold back some of the rights (including the more lucrative ones) that the publisher might otherwise have been able to persuade the author to give up. Payments (fees, royalties and advances) will almost certainly be higher, and publishers need to be more punctilious in their record-keeping and prompt in their payments. The relationship between the author and the publisher may suffer in all this, but the growing power and importance of the agent has added a new and revitalizing element to the publishing network.

Agents have taken on additional intermediary roles such as e-publishing and the promotion of clients for speaking engagements, and they are likely to continue to expand into other sectors of the media industry.

Literary consultancies

In addition to the fact that the authors of children's fiction and non-fiction books are unlikely to find a publisher without having the support of an agent, many agents prefer authors who have been recommended to them by a literary consultancy, a new type of gatekeeper that has emerged in recent years.

Literary consultancies charge fees for workshops, plot advice, supply critical reader's reports, and help with putting together publishing proposals. These consultancies also charge a commission (around 10%) if they are successful in placing the author's work with an agent, which means that the trawling that used to be done by publishers and then by literary agents is now sometimes being done by a third level of gatekeepers. This is at the budding author's expense, but an increasing number accept that there are additional hurdles to jump and additional up-front costs to bear.

The effect of agents on publishing

As other people (literary agents and consultancies) take on some of the tasks previously undertaken by editors in trade publishing, the publisher's role is being redefined. The publisher or commissioning editor continues to be responsible for developing publishing projects that will fulfil the expectations of the company's sales, marketing and finance departments. However, this is done not, as previously, solely by developing a publishing programme or stable of authors from scratch, but also by judiciously acquiring rights from other intermediaries. Consultants and agents, who are in touch with a wide range of potential publishers in major markets around the world, have often already cultivated these works. Some publishers hire literary scouts to seek out titles published in other countries and languages that may be suitable for them to publish in a local edition. Literary translators are also influential in recommending books to publishers.

'Being involved in every stage of putting together a non-fiction book proposal, offering substantial editing on fiction manuscripts, and coming up with book ideas for authors looking for their next project is as much a part of our work as selling, negotiating contracts, and collecting monies for our clients. We follow a book from its inception through its sale to a publisher, its publication, and beyond. Our commitment to our writers does not, by any means, end when we have collected our commission.'

Dystel & Goderich Literary Management, New York

The author's identity

The process of mentoring an author, and the intervention of a number of different people in the development of a title, mean that the publication that is eventually offered for sale is not just the written work. The publication package includes the brand identity of the author – his or her future potential value as an income generator. This can make the risk of a high advance and a multi-book contract worth entering into. The author, whether a 'celebrity' or an 'expert' (hopefully articulate and good looking enough for TV – or engagingly offensive), can be a major component of the marketing mix. Authors are encouraged to create personal brands, their own 'platforms', which enable them to develop other income-generating activities (personal appearances, magazine articles, TV and radio spots, merchandise, and training programmes). Consultancies, agents and publishers encourage authors to build up such a portfolio approach to self-promotion through the use of social media.

This is not just true at a mass-market level: academic authors, politicians, and other professionals find it difficult to get an enthusiastic and committed agent or publisher if they cannot first demonstrate that they have a status outside of their narrow specialist field, and are able to communicate this expertise and can come across engagingly in the wider media. The publication of a successful book (hopefully the beginning of a successful series of publications and adaptations in other media) also contributes to the professional standing of the authors, and pays back to the author, agent and publisher in terms of increased sales and profit.

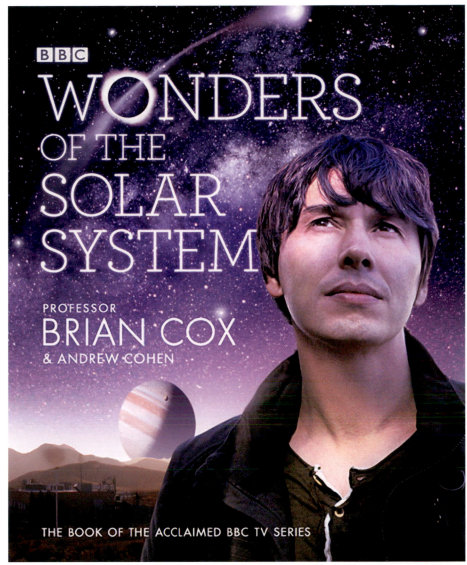

3.3

3.3
Brian Cox
Professor Brian Cox is a physicist who has successfully combined an academic career with writing popular books and presenting TV programmes on science, in particular astronomy. This book is published by HarperCollins.

Discussion questions

1. Why do authors use agents?

2. How is the role of agents changing?

3. What is the difference between an author's agent and a literary consultancy?

4. What is an author's platform?

Networks and opinion formers

Changes in the means and nature of communication, with an increasing number of channels available, means that there are now lots of new ways to disseminate information about publishing products and services. The communication and promotion to potential readers is part of a publishing communications network, using an ever-increasing variety of media and methods to create 'buzz' and word-of-mouth recommendation.

How to make a bestseller
This chart shows some of the factors that can contribute to the success of a book.

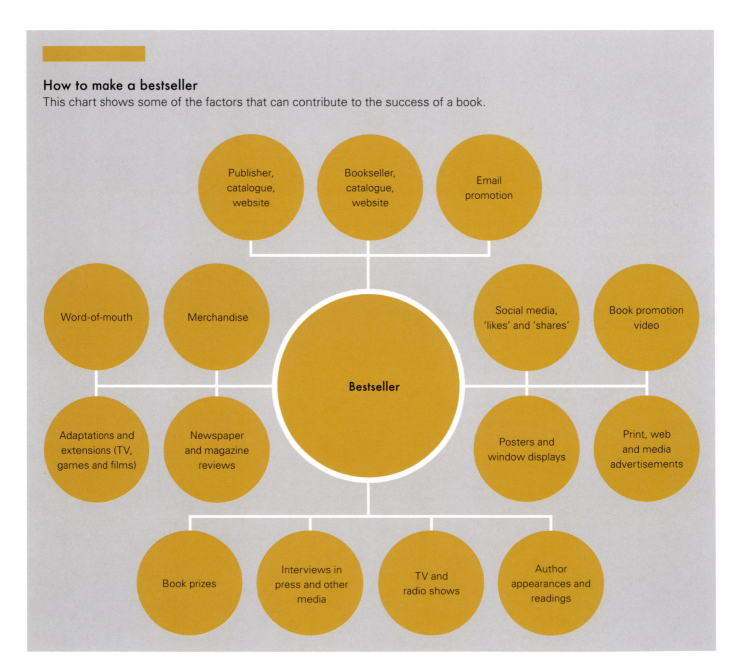

3.4

Anthony Horowitz
With a career that covers writing novels, films, TV shows and plays, Anthony Horowitz is a good example of a writer who works across the media. He has created a portfolio that attracts a broad fan base similar to other non-writing celebrities. Here he is with young readers at the Hong Kong Book Fair.

3.4

3.5

3.5

Jacqueline Wilson
Children's authors have some of the most engaging websites. These young 'digital natives' are used to navigating quite complex sites, and children's publisher and author websites need lots of activities to engage them: sticky content that keeps them on the site and returning for more.

Word-of-mouth and self-promotion

The concepts behind 'word-of-mouth' are applicable to any professional and specialist network in which people talk to each other and make recommendations, and personal recommendation is often cited as the most important way to ensure success in publishing. We tend to trust messages from our friends and family (or a trusted brand), and recommendations from these trusted sources are more convincing than a promotion sent by someone we don't know. Self-promotion is managed through the judicious use of social media, which can give a direct, authentic, voice to the author. Most authors have their own websites, and many have blogs, and use social networking tools with which they seek to build an online identity. Some consultants and entrepreneurs have recognized that authors are often not adept at such self-promotion and have developed businesses to help authors in this demanding task.

Creating publicity also entails author appearances, interviews (managed of course by the publicity department or agency), readings in bookshops, at festivals, on podcasts and in other digital media.

Prizes

Prizes play a significant role in book promotion. Big annual prizes include the Man Booker Prize in the UK, the Prix Goncourt in France, and the International IMPAC Dublin Literary Award. In the US, winning a Pulitzer Prize can be a big boost to any writer's career, and in Canada the Governor General's Literary Awards attract national interest in both Francophone and Anglophone writing.

There are many other prizes for writers, translators, illustrators and publishers, and while some carry significant prize money, the real value to the author and publisher is often in the increased sales that result from the publicity surrounding the winner of one of the big prizes.

Prizes often cause controversy, which can also help sales. One example of such controversy was the award of the biennial Man Booker International Prize to Philip Roth in 2011. One of the judges, Carmen Callil, resigned from the panel and criticized the award of the prize to the famous American author saying: 'He goes on and on and on about the same subject in almost every single book. It's as though he's sitting on your face and you can't breathe.' Needless to say the controversy led to extensive press, radio and TV coverage.

3.6
Oprah's Book Club
Oprah Winfrey started her book club on her TV show in 1996. The show was influential in promoting the sale of selected contemporary novels by writers such as Toni Morrison, as well as some classics by authors such as John Steinbeck. Oprah's Book Club is now part of Oprah's Next Chapter.

'The negotiation between marketplace, counting house and the literary and intellectual environment is perennial in the publishing industry and so, as an adjunct to the industry, literary prizes are subject to those negotiations too. Literary prizes frequently intend to reward literary value – to fulfil "the demands of excellence" – but can also have the effect of increasing sales and promoting business.'

Professor Claire Squires, writing in Javnost – The Public: Journal of the European Institute for Communication and Culture

3.6

Traditional review media

Reviews in newspapers, magazines and on radio and TV have always played an important role in helping potential readers to identify and evaluate new books that might be of interest to them. Publishers still go to great lengths to solicit good reviews, but the nature of these reviews is changing. Many daily and weekly titles no longer have a literary editor responsible just for book reviews, and reviews are often linked to what is called 'off-the-page' selling through newspaper e-commerce sites such as the Guardian Book Shop.

More and more coverage of books is celebrity driven and the interview or exposé is now the stock-in-trade of book coverage in the media. Literary editors, and the digital media gatekeepers (for example, bloggers and tweeters with lots of followers) who are replacing them, are successful if they are trusted, and their recommendations become known, circulated and further recommended among a wider circle of readers. This is as true for educational, academic and STM publications as for trade fiction. Getting a positive review on a specialist blog, website or publication is a hugely valuable way of reaching a niche readership. However, the authority, reliability and impartiality of some reviews are now in question due to the predominance of advertorial comment (something that looks impartial but is actually paid for like advertising), as well as online reader reviews, and cross-media promotion orchestrated by a cultural elite.

Reading clubs, both in the home and in the media, are a significant way in which books are promoted. Publishers promote their books for book club readership and TV and radio media have played their part. Oprah in the US and Richard and Judy in the UK were able to generate enough buzz for book recommendations made in their TV shows to create instant bestsellers.

Promotion buzz is not a new thing

'The publisher had hoped for this. Mr Jedwood was an energetic and sanguine man, who had entered upon his business with a determination to rival in a year or so the houses which had slowly risen into commanding stability. He had no great capital, but the stroke of fortune that had wedded him to a popular novelist enabled him to count on steady profit from one source, and boundless faith in his own judgement urged him to an initial outlay which made the prudent shake their heads.

He talked much of "the new era", foresaw revolutions in publishing and book-selling, planned every week a score of untried ventures which should appeal to the democratic generation just maturing; in the meantime, was ready to publish anything which seemed likely to get talked about.'
George Gissing, *New Grub Street*, 1891 (This is a fictional account of someone creating a 'buzz'.)

Discussion questions

1. What are the best ways to generate word-of-mouth publicity?

2. Why are literary prizes important?

3. How have book reviews changed in the digital publishing world?

4. What factors can be important in creating a bestseller?

Channels to readers and buyers

Producing the best book in the world is pointless if nobody reads it. You must have the ability to communicate with the people who want it and have a channel through which it can reach the customers at the right time, in the right quantity, and at a price that they find acceptable. The role of distributors and bookshops in this process is changing and there are many new kinds of supply services being developed that bring new types of business model to the greater publishing network.

Communication and supply channels

Communication channels and supply channels have fundamentally changed in the digital culture. Communication and supply now take place at all hours of the day and night; they happen across time zones and national boundaries. Every transaction entails an evaluation by the customer of comparative cost, speed, convenience and the likelihood of satisfying personal expectations. People have needs that are increasingly time sensitive and are immediately validated (or not) by real and virtual social network pressures. Book buyers, like consumers of all kinds, have grown accustomed to being able to choose from a huge range of options. Their needs can often be met by any number of services providing possible solutions.

The way publications are acquired has changed. In the decade after 2000, publishing waited for what was termed its 'iPod moment' similar to the revolution that happened in the music industry with the invention of iTunes. That moment came with the Kindle, the iPad, and the Nook. These devices and the supply chains that provide them with content have brought the e-book into the mainstream. Publishers continue to look to the music industry for innovation models. For example, the idea of 'playlists' of texts is being developed as a new way of delivering customized selections of text; something that could be particularly useful for publications such as cookery books and travel guides.

Cloud-based streaming services have been launched to provide an e-book service offering publications at low or no cost in return for the reader's acceptance that their reading will be interrupted by advertising messages.

Rental services (for both trade books and textbooks) have also been developed. Library lending of physical books, already under threat in cash-strapped public sector libraries, is being replaced by e-lending (both through formal, library-like services, and on a more informal basis) as a feature of book supply.

In the end, effective publishing distribution depends on two words: *availability* and *display*. The ways in which we get information on and obtain publications in the digital age may be different, but the fundamental principles remain the same.

3.7
Amanda Hocking
Torn is the second
book in the *Trylle
Trilogy.* It was first
self-published as an
e-book. Hocking sold
1.5 million e-books
without any help
from a publisher in
20 months starting
in April 2010. She
made $2.5 million
(£1.59 million) and
unsurprisingly secured
a book deal.

3.7

Self-publishing

Publishing's major activity is to manage
the transformation of an author's words
and images in such a way that they fit
the requirements of a market. Digital
technology enables more people to
develop new platforms for their work,
and has given further encouragement
to the idea that 'everyone has a book
inside them'. After decades when it
became harder and harder for aspiring
authors to find a publisher to take them
on, there has been an explosive growth
in the number of writers and artists
publishing their own work using POD
technology, or self-publishing on the
Internet. The growth in such output
accelerated in 2009 when over 750,000
self-published e-books appeared in
the US, and it continues at a rapid
rate (*Publishers Weekly*, 2010).

For the vast majority, self-publishing
might be a source of some personal
fulfilment, but it is very different from
mainstream commercial publishing.
Many self-published authors have
limited appreciation of the genre they
are trying to write for, and often do not
have the language and editing skills
to produce marketable texts. They
also rarely have, and find it difficult
to create, the network connections that
publishers have to publicize and promote
their work. Only a small handful of
authors, such as Amanda Hocking
(author of the *My Blood Approves* series
and the *Trylle Trilogy*), has achieved
star quality publicity and spectacular
sales. In 2011 Hocking signed a much-
publicized, four-book deal with
traditional publisher Pan Macmillan.

Indie publishing

The commercial need of big publishing companies to satisfy shareholder demands means that they are increasingly choosing to invest heavily in fewer titles, so, with an increased number of people trying to become published writers, many are unable to find either a publisher or an agent who will work on their behalf. Personal computers enable authors to design and produce publications themselves, and this combined with affordable POD and e-book distribution has created an explosion of self-publication.

Developments in POD have caused costs to reduce and improved the availability of colour POD and different formats and bindings. Customers no longer perceive these books as inferior to books produced on litho presses. These factors encouraged the self-publishing of more physical books to develop alongside self-published e-books.

The self-publishing phenomenon is increasingly known as independent (or 'indie') publishing. With services like Kindle Direct Publishing, you can self-publish books on the Amazon Kindle Store. Under the Kindle arrangements, the author of self-published books can get up to a 70 per cent royalty and the books are available for purchase on Kindle devices and Kindle apps for iPad, iPhone, iPod touch, PC, Mac, Blackberry, and Android-based devices. Other companies that provide these types of service are Lulu, and Barnes & Noble PubIt!

'The ease with which you can self-publish your own work (or set up as a publisher and publish other people's) has had an unfortunate side-effect, and that's to hugely increase the amount of poorly produced work which is available.'

David Moody, quoted in 'How self-publishing came of age' by Alison Flood, the Guardian, *2011*

The degree to which indie publishers are successful is, as with all publishers, dependent on the extent to which they can develop their publishing networks, and market their wares through all the viral mechanisms available. Just as commercial publishers saw the publishing opportunities that arose from the blogosphere – repackaging blogs as both p- and e-books – the possibilities of exploiting the boom in self-publishing are not being overlooked; and commercial publishers look out for promising 'indie' titles to repackage and publish for a wider market. There are also some modern-day vanity publishers, which act as facilitators for authors who want to self-publish – still charging a fee of course.

Self-publishing is also developing as a major publishing channel for academic and scholarly work, often through programmes in institutions. The eScholarship service at the University of California is one example of an institution providing a suite of open access scholarly publishing services and research tools. This enables departments, research units, publishing programmes, and individual scholars associated with the University of California to have direct control over the creation and dissemination of their work.

Kirkus Indie

Both the literary avant-garde and the mainstream now take self-publishing seriously.

For over 70 years Kirkus Reviews has provided critical, descriptive, and concise reviews of forthcoming books in a twice-monthly publication. Now Kirkus produces Kirkus Indie to review titles from indie publishers. The reviews normally appear two or three months prior to publication. A review in Kirkus is often the first review of a book to appear anywhere, and a good many books may receive no other notice than the one they get in Kirkus (or similar services such as BlueInk Reviews).

Vanity publishing

There have always been people who have paid for the production of publications that they have written or otherwise wanted to see published outside of the usual commercial publishing channels. Companies called vanity publishers (a term which arose in the US in the 1920s), publish works for a fee. They prospered in the twentieth century by offering such services to aspiring authors who could not find a publisher to take them on.

There are still companies that will publish books for a fee, and in some instances, such as when a family wants to publish a family history for their own use and enjoyment, they may have a legitimate place. However, some of the services these companies offer are inadequate, and, as a result, give limited satisfaction to their customers.

Discussion questions

1. What are some of the reasons for the growth in self-publishing?

2. Why do some self-published books get taken on by traditional commercial publishers?

3. How has POD contributed to the growth of indie publishing?

4. How is self-publishing used to publish different types of books?

Case study:

Frankfurt

Book Fair

The Frankfurt Book Fair began more than 500 years ago, shortly after Gutenberg established his press in nearby Mainz. After the seventeenth century, its importance was overtaken by the Book Fair in Leipzig, another important publishing city in Germany. It was not until 1949, with Leipzig behind the Iron Curtain in the German Democratic Republic, that the Frankfurt Book Fair was re-established.

Now, for nearly a week every year in October, the publishing community gathers at the Frankfurt Book Fair – the world's most important marketplace for books, media, rights and licences in the world. Publishers, booksellers, agents, designers, film producers, authors and a host of industry organizations and independent consultants come together to learn what's happening in the world of publishing. They meet clients, customers and publishing partners, and develop and nurture the networks that are essential to their work. Altogether there are more than 7,000 exhibitors from more than 100 countries, about 300,000 visitors and over 10,000 journalists.

The exhibitors and visitors are not just from the various sectors of the book industry, but also other related industries such as film, games, and information and communications technology. New areas of specialization – from digital publishing services and computer games production, to legal and financial consultants for cross-media products – are now found at the Book Fair. There are numerous international training and networking events, including major conferences organized by the Frankfurt Academy, such as StoryDrive and the Tools of Change in 2011.

3.8
Guest of honour
New Zealand was selected to be guest of honour at the Frankfurt Book Fair in 2012. This provided an opportunity for the guest nation to promote both the cultural and commercial interests of its literary and publishing communities, and encourages international collaborations between the guest and the host nations.

3.8

Every year the Frankfurt Book Fair has a particular country focus. In recent years the Guests of Honour have been Argentina (2010), Iceland (2011), and New Zealand (2012).

Frankfurt is very significant for the international rights and licences trade; it has a special Literary Agents and Scouts Centre (LitAg). In spite of the ease of modern telecommunication, teleconferencing and instantaneous data transfer, publishers still like to meet up and discuss books.

'The more globalized the books business becomes, the greater is everyone's need to meet in person at least once a year – and that, of course, is in Frankfurt. Conversations about people and books are indispensable.'

Professor Gottfried Honnefelder, President of the Association of German Publishers and Booksellers

3.9

3.9
Frankfurt Book Fair
Hundreds of thousands of people visit the Frankfurt Book Fair. In recent years the comic zone has been a popular draw for the German public, with many exhibitors and visitors wearing elaborate character costumes (cosplay).

Key points

The Frankfurt Book Fair is one of the most exciting and vibrant events in the publishing calendar. With such a vast gathering of diverse interests, it is impossible to describe everything that might happen, but most of the activities can be seen as helping publishing professionals to develop and reinforce their membership of and influence in networks that are important to their business and their career.

- Selling and buying rights is what Frankfurt is all about for many agents, publishers, and an increasing array of other creative industry specialists. During the day, rights managers will have back-to-back meetings to introduce rights partners to new projects, check on the progress of current contracts, and keep up to date on what's in demand in different world markets. Even though communication in the digital world is now constant and immediate, personal contact and after-hours 'schmoozing' are still essential for the development of trust and business relationships.

- Sales people also have a full schedule, meeting booksellers and distributors from around the world – all under one roof. Frankfurt provides opportunities to talk about new books with your Indian representatives, negotiate discounts with a German importer, develop a promotional campaign with your Japanese sales agent, and track down customers who are being slow in settling their accounts. One trip to Frankfurt can avoid thousands of miles of costly and time-consuming travel, something that is also possible at other big book fairs like the London Book Fair and BookExpo America.

- Everyone responsible for business development, from web managers and publicity supremos to commissioning editors and logistic directors, are in Frankfurt picking up on the latest trends.

- Frankfurt has a very full programme of conferences, seminars and other events that cover key markets, publishing trends and new technology.

- Many book fairs do not admit members of the public, but there are special public opening hours at the Frankfurt Book Fair. This means that this is also a major German cultural event with hundreds of thousands of non-professional visitors, great media interest, and an opportunity for German publishers and authors to promote their books directly to the public.

Activity

Imagine you are an editor, agent, or rights manager going to this year's Frankfurt Book Fair. Look at the Frankfurt website and make a list of the things that you would plan to do during the fair.

1. How would you use the event to find out about new authors and book titles that might be suitable for your own publishing programme?

2. What would you do to identify publishing trends that would help you to plan your company's activities over the coming years?

3. What can you discover about digital publishing developments in other parts of the world that might be applicable to your own company's activities?

4. Why is the Guest of Honour Programme an important part of the Frankfurt Book Fair?

Chapter 4

Editorial

processes

This chapter examines how publishers decide what to publish; how they acquire publishing properties and commission authors to write new publications; and how editors research the market using formal tools and informal networks. It also looks at the process of editing a book from submission to publication, and how editors deal with other people inside and outside their own publishing organization.

What the publisher decides to publish is called the publisher's list, and this is usually developed according to a plan with a specific market niche in mind. While many publishers have what appear to be quite similar lists (for example, travel publishers such as Lonely Planet and Rough Guides), each has its own publishing policy and publishing plan that defines its identity to both potential authors and to the market.

The publisher must make sure that its publishing programme is good not only for the publisher's reputation but also for its bottom line, so we also look briefly at the basic economics of publishing. The chapter examines the publisher–author contract, which is central to the publishing relationship. It also explores how new formats and digital platforms are changing how publishers deal with territorial and language rights.

Policy and planning: list building and market niches

Publishing, like other creative industries, is based on discovering, nurturing and refining the talents of creative people, and then exposing them to a market audience in a way that ensures that both author and publisher get an adequate return on the time and money that they have invested.

The strategic purpose of the list

When publishers look for authors and books to publish, they need a plan. No publisher would survive for long by publishing too many different types of book within one list or under one imprint. This is why larger publishers have several lists (with different imprints) to publish books for different markets, and they even preserve the brand identity of lists that they acquire (for example, Knopf, Virago, and Churchill Livingstone).

One publishing brand or imprint would find it hard to handle a cookery book one week, a treatise on nuclear energy the next, and an illustrated children's story about a polka dot whale the week after. While each book may be excellent, the publisher would not have the skills and resources to develop, produce, promote and distribute such varied titles to diverse audiences in a way that would make economic sense.

Publishers specialize in particular types of publishing (such as trade, educational, academic, or children's), but within these broad publishing areas they also build lists of titles that are targeted towards specific market niches. The non-fiction trade publisher might have a strong list of literary biographies; the educational publisher might focus on geography books for secondary students; the academic publisher might have a world-leading list of books on film or fashion; and a children's publisher might be best known for illustrated books featuring inner-city life.

Developing a new list represents a major commitment of resources (people, time, and financial investment), so the management of the publishing company need to be convinced not only that there is a market for the proposed list development, but also that the company is in a position to compete.

Creating a list that is close to the existing publishing programme can build on current knowledge of the market. It represents a lower risk than developing a list in an area that is totally new to the publisher.

A SWOT analysis (Strengths, Weaknesses, Opportunities and Threats) may well form part of the new list research, in which the company's capabilities, resources and experience in relation to the list (its strengths and weaknesses) are examined and evaluated, as well as the possibilities the development may represent (the opportunities) and possible risks (threats) to the success of the business.

The decision to develop a new list is made by the senior management team. The senior managers must feel confident that the company has the skills and resources needed to make a success of publishing in a particular subject area, and that it will be profitable for the company to use these skills and resources in this way.

Once the go-ahead decision is made, the development of the new list is the responsibility of an individual publisher or editorial director, and is managed throughout the publishing process by a commissioning (US: acquisitions, or sponsoring) editor. In some cases, the company will recruit a new editor with specific, relevant experience, and a demonstrable track record in managing a list in a new business area.

'I have considerable experience in making wrong decisions. It is a necessary rite of passage in the building of a great publishing house.'

Alan Hill, In Pursuit of Publishing, *1988
(Former chairman and managing director
of Heinemann Educational Books)*

Decision matrix

As an aid to making decisions on whether or not to publish, it is helpful to have certain criteria in mind. One way to structure the evaluation of a project is by using a decision matrix like this simple template on the right. A tool like this can help the publisher to identify early on if a given title will be suitable for their publishing programme, and act as a counterbalance to a publisher's enthusiasm and optimism.

On the opposite page is a completed matrix with some information on a new fashion design list. Would you consider this a good list for the company to develop?

Project:	Positives (+) and negatives (-)				
Criterion	++ (very positive)	+ (positive)	+/– (positive or negative)	– (negative)	– – (very negative)
Growth market					
Competition					
Author reputation, reliability and platform					
Access to market					
Competitive position					
Design and production capabilities (print and digital)					
Investment and risk					

Publishing lists, seasonal lists and mailing lists

Building a list in the publishing sense means creating a coherent publishing programme (as in the Penguin list) or a specific list within the overall programme of the publishing company. In developing a specific list (and titles within that list) the publisher also considers whether the books to be published will have a long sales life and become part of a backlist that will sustain the company for years to come, or whether they will only sell for a short time as new (front list) titles. The possibility that a title may be a strong backlist title may influence the decision to invest in the project.

Publishers may also refer to their seasonal list; these are the titles due for release in spring and autumn/fall (or for the Christmas market) that are announced in a seasonal catalogue. This seasonal list often identifies projects that the publisher considers its lead titles; the ones for which it has high hopes and to which it may have allocated additional promotional resources.

Project: New Fashion Design List	Positives (+) and negatives (-)				
Criterion	++	+	+/-	-	- -
Growth market: *Many new courses in UK and US*	++				
Competition: *Major publisher in this field has big market share but has not kept list up to date*	++				
Author reputation, reliability and platform: *Younger lecturers looking for a publisher who is receptive to new approaches to subject*		+			
Access to market: *Some overlap with current market, but need to develop promotional tools for fashion departments at art schools*			+/-		
Competitive position: *Will be competing against a market leader*			+/-		
Design and production capabilities (print and digital): *Can prepare list that is far more attractive to market in terms of design and production quality*	++				
Investment and risk: *Moderately high investment required, but possibility of taking over market leadership position in 3–5 years*		+			

4.1

4.1
Christmas gift books
Christmas is a major selling period for trade books. Many books are bought as gifts, and seasonal promotions are conducted by publishers and booksellers, such as Foyles in London.

Discussion questions

1. How important is it to plan a new list in terms of the income and profit a publisher expects to make?

2. What is a SWOT analysis used for?

3. Which departments are involved in the list development process?

4. What is a seasonal list?

Commissioning: research, reputation and funds

Acquisition, commissioning and list building are at the foundation of publishing. The decision to commit time and resources to a publishing programme is made on the basis of the best available knowledge and advice. However, no publishing project, and particularly the development of a whole range of titles for a particular audience, is risk-free. In order to manage this 'risk-taking' element of publishing, the commissioning/acquisition must be undertaken with care, skill, confidence and impeccable attention to detail.

Acquisition and commissioning titles

Deciding what to publish is best done on the basis of a structured publishing plan, for which particular books and authors are recruited. *The Publishing Business*, for example, was planned as part of the AVA publishing list, and an author was then recruited to write a specific book for an identified market.

Editors are the first to research the market for proposed publications. They do this using their own contacts, authors and editorial advisors, and by consulting on an informal and formal basis with the sales and marketing department. The research looks at the publisher's own sales for books on similar subjects and at industry statistics available, including reports from Nielsen BookScan (see page 182).

Publishers try to quantify the size of the specific market, and assess the competition. Market knowledge, and the position the publisher wishes to take in respect to the market, also determines the tone to be taken, and the viewpoint from which the book will be written. A publisher of sports biographies, for example, will have clear ideas about whether a new book should be a respectful and measured life history of a sporting legend, or a chatty fan-friendly promotion for a current sports personality.

Decisions: the publishing proposal

As we saw briefly in Chapter 3, professionally managed publishing houses plan their publishing programme with more or less formal publishing proposals. Many publishers are quite specific about the sort of information that must be included in the publishing proposal if it is to be considered by their publishing company, some of the most common are listed here in the 'Reasons to publish' box.

Reasons to publish

At the development stage the editor will need to consider the following questions:

1. Why is there a need for the book and how will it be different from other books already available?
2. Are there reasons why this is a good time to publish a book of this type?
3. Who will want to read the book, and how will these people acquire or otherwise gain access to it?
4. How large is the market?
5. What will be in the book, and how will it be organized in various chapters? Will there be illustrations, other information and features?
6. Will the book be suitable for adaptation to other formats?
7. Why is the author the right person to write the book? Does he or she have a reputation and a network in the specialist area? Has the author already written successfully on this subject?

Creating a brand for a series

Fiction publishers like series of books that have a common main character. This is particularly true of crime fiction where the author and character brands are reinforced with each new title, sometimes building on the popularity of TV adaptations. To some extent, the works of popular crime fiction authors become sub-lists in their own right. The Inspector Zen series by Michael Dibdin has been so successful that some of the books have been adapted for TV. This cover stresses the brand of the series and the author. It reminds us of the central character and conjures up the atmosphere of its Rome location as seen on TV. It also discreetly shows the publisher's logo.

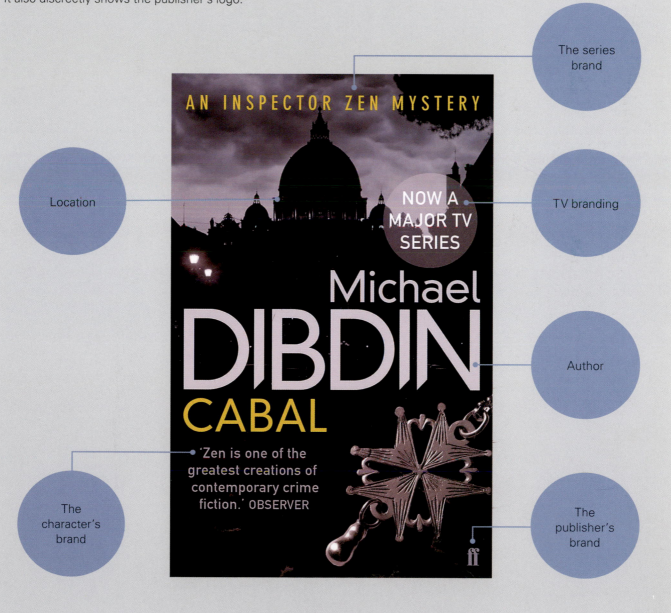

The series brand

Location

TV branding

Author

The character's brand

The publisher's brand

AN INSPECTOR ZEN MYSTERY

NOW A MAJOR TV SERIES

Michael DIBDIN

CABAL

'Zen is one of the greatest creations of contemporary crime fiction.' OBSERVER

4.2
Julie Powell
Julie Powell wrote a blog about her attempt to cook all the recipes in Julia Child's *Mastering the Art of French Cooking*. The blog was popular and was published as a book by Little, Brown and Company. It then became a successful film *Julie and Julia* starring Meryl Streep.

4.2

Publication dates

Proposed publication dates for titles in the list must be planned, depending on the nature of the market. A university textbook needs to be published in time to be evaluated for adoption for next year's courses; a guidebook must be available in time for the peak tourist season; and a Christmas gift book should be in the shops by October, to catch the seasonal selling period in November and December.

The length of time for stock of printed books to reach the market must also be considered. When the time to receive inventory from the printer (very possibly in Asia), and ship them to retail customers is added to the schedule, the total time needed to get the books to market can be lengthened by at least several weeks, if not months.

Sifting through the new slush pile

As we've already seen, the possibilities offered by digital tools and the Internet have created a publishing environment in which writers sometimes think that they can do the job themselves, and that there is no longer a need for the publisher. This may be true in some cases, but even the briefest look at many self-publications on the World Wide Web proves that this is not usually so. The vast majority of tweets, blogs and self-published e-books remain unread by anyone but the author and a few close associates.

This may be because it is often easy for readers to judge the quality of both content and form, and it is clear that quality comes from the effective use of expert skills and experience. Good publishers are the custodians of high quality in publishing, and the system functions more effectively when different parts of the process are undertaken by specialists.

The publisher's decisions on authorship, design, and marketing create a publishing package that is in all respects suitable for the proposed readership, and is created with an eye to the whole marketing mix, and this remains true with digital publications.

Therefore, when a successful writer of a blog or self-published title is recruited by professional publishers to produce a publication through more traditional channels, it enables the author to extend his or her 'platform' and readership. The publisher develops the idea as a marketable property for which a readership has already been identified, by a writer (such as Julie Powell), who has already proved able to communicate with that audience.

'A literary creation is thus not considered an intrinsic "work-in-progress", never closed, never definitive, arrested at the moment of publication ("We publish to stop revising," declared the Mexican writer Alfonso Reyes), but as a more or less all-rounded product initiated by the writer, finished off by an editor, and approved by various specialists in marketing and sales.'

Alberto Manguel, The City of Words, *2008*

Doing your homework and getting the right advice

Publishers cannot rely just on authors and their agents to tell them how good a work is. Editors responsible for commissioning and acquisition need to be knowledgeable about the area in which they are working. They must attend specialist meetings, conferences and seminars to get information and to keep in touch with relevant networks. Sometimes an advisory board will be created to help keep the editor up to date with the field and to assist in planning the list, and editors often send out proposals and manuscripts for specialist 'peer review', feedback and recommendations.

Publishers interested in developing publications programmes that include works translated from other languages will also keep in contact with trusted translators, who may be among the first to know about a promising writer working in another language.

If the success of a particular list depends on knowledge of specific parts of the supply chain or collaboration with other media companies, then the editor will need to keep in touch with these while developing the list. He or she will also need an awareness of major events like the Olympic Games, museum exhibitions or national elections, if they are relevant to the marketability of a title.

Financial viability

Before the decision to publish is made, it is the editor's responsibility to show that the project is financially viable (this task may also be undertaken by others, such as the publisher). This requires pulling together a lot of information, making certain assumptions based on experience and expertise, and consulting widely within the company and with external experts. This is important because the publishing company pays for the cost of producing a publication up front. It may take more than a year from the start of commissioning a project before the publisher begins to get a return on the financial investment.

By making comparisons with sales of similar titles, the editor estimates how many copies may be sold over what time period. It is important to consider the product life cycle of the publication, as this determines how quickly the project generates income to pay its costs. There is a big difference, for example, between the short life of most new trade titles and the long-term possibilities of a successful college textbook, and this is important in judging the publishing risk.

A preliminary price is set for each format – physical book (hardback and/or paperback) and e-book – and the price of any other materials that may accompany the publication. The optimum price must fit in with market expectations, the price of comparative titles, and the production values and quality of the publication. Pricing strategies may also include 'bundles'; for example when a printed textbook or reference work may be 'bundled' and sold with online access to other resources.

The income the publisher may receive is estimated. In order to do this effectively, the editor must understand how discounts to booksellers or commissions to sales agents reduce the amount the publisher actually gets for the sale of each book. The sum that remains is the Net Sales Revenue (NSR) or Net Receipts. The publisher uses this money to pay for the publishing costs and provide some profit for the owners or investors.

The publisher (with input from the editor and the marketing and sales departments) also calculates the direct costs necessary to publish and promote the publication. This includes payments to the author, either as a royalty (with or without an advance payment) or as a fee. The editor also obtains an estimate of the production costs from the production department. Other direct costs of promotion and publicity are also included in the calculation. The total of these costs is deducted from the estimated income (NSR) to calculate whether the publication will make the required contribution to the firm's overheads and satisfy profit requirements.

Lastly, but often critically important to the overall viability of the publishing project, the editor will consult with the company's rights department, other publishers within the publishing group, and other industry contacts to see if the publication has other rights income potential.

This financial information is used by the editor (along with information about the proposed publication, its market, and its importance to the company) to obtain the support of senior management, and to get approval to go ahead with the project.

Profit and loss account

At an early stage in a project's development, a basic profit and loss account (P&L) is prepared to evaluate the financial viability of a title. Here is a simple example.

	Unit in currency	% of RRP	% of NSR
Title: Fashion Careers	£/$/€		
P&L per copy			
Recommended Retail Price (RRP) (also called cover or list price)	12.50	100%	
Average discount for bookseller	6.25	50%	
Net Sales Revenue (NSR) (receipts)	6.25	50%	100%
Unit production cost (the total estimated production costs of the print run divided by the number of units printed)	2.50	20%	40%
Author royalty	0.625	5%	10%
Gross profit/margin	3.13	25%	50%
P&L for print run			
Income			
Sales of 4,200 @ NSR of 6.25 each	26,250		100%
Returns of 500 copies (10% of print run) (damaged/unsold copies)	0		0%
300 review, inspection, desk copies (6%)	0		0%
Expenditure			
5,000 copies printed @ 2.50 each	12,500		48%
Royalty on 4,200 copies	2,625		10%
Gross profit	**11,125**		**42%**

Discussion questions

1. Why is it important to understand why people tend to buy certain types of book?

2. How can an editor get management approval for a new list or new title?

3. What should a publishing proposal include?

4. What is Net Sales Revenue (NSR)?

Contractual matters: formats and co-editions

The contract between the author and the publisher is at the core of publishing, as it sets out the detailed terms of their relationship. Publishers usually have their own standard contract into which the agreed terms are inserted, and the commissioning/acquisitions editor is generally responsible for negotiating these. As the final contract is a legally binding agreement, it is signed by a publisher or company director on behalf of the publishing company. There may be cases where issues of potential libel or other legal issues may require the firm's legal officers to approve the contract and, rarely, even the manuscript.

While the specific terms may differ, all publishing contracts contain the following information:

◉ Details of the parties to the agreement (publisher, author), the book's working title (the final title is often chosen at a later date), the proposed length of the book, and the expected date that the author will deliver the full text to the publisher (and the digital and physical form in which it will be supplied).

◉ Details of the rights granted to the publisher by the author (including who holds copyright), and the territories and formats for which the publisher will have these rights.

◉ The author warrants the work will be original, and will not contain anything that is libellous, defamatory or illegal. The author may also agree not to write something similar for another publisher.

◉ The contract covers the payments to be made to the author, including any fees, royalties and advances, and payments for any subsidiary rights sold by the publisher. It also covers how and when payments will be made.

◉ Finally the contract will specify how long the contract will last for, and how any disputes will be handled.

Editors don't need to be legal experts, but they do need to understand the importance of having a clear, well-constructed contract that covers the agreement that they are making with an author. And they need to be able to explain this clearly to the author, so that the editor-author relationship develops in an atmosphere of trust.

A publisher's contract with an author is a legally binding agreement that should be clearly expressed and cover all areas of possible future misunderstanding about respective responsibilities and benefits.

An example of a publisher's contract

This sample contract shows some of the most important parts of a contract, although there are likely to be more clauses as required by the publisher, the author or the agent.

AGREEMENT

made this <<day number>> day of <<month>>, <<year>> between <<Author's name>> of <<Author's address>> (hereinafter called the Author); and <<Publisher's name>> of <Publisher's principal place of business> (hereinafter called the Publisher);

GRANT

In consideration of the payment hereafter described, the author hereby grants and assigns to the Publisher the sole and exclusive rights to publish the Work now entitled <<Title of book>> (hereinafter called the Work), in all forms including print, digital and electronic, in all territories of the world and in all languages.

REPRESENTATIONS AND WARRANTIES

The Author represents that he/she is the sole proprietor of the Work, that the Work is original, and to the best of his/her knowledge that the Work does not contain any libellous matter, does not violate the civil rights of any person or persons, does not infringe any existing copyright and has not heretofore been published in book form.

DELIVERY

The Author agrees to deliver to the publisher by <<Date>>, a complete typewritten script of between <<Number of words>> and <<Number of words>> as well as a complete electronic text of the Work in a format to be determined by the Publisher (hereinafter called the Manuscript). If the Manuscript shall not have been delivered within three (3) months after the date specified in this agreement the Publisher may, at its option, terminate this agreement by notice in writing posted or delivered to the Author.

PUBLICATION

The Publisher agrees to publish the Work in book form at its own expense not later than 12 months after the delivery of the completed Work. All decisions relating to the editing, design, production and marketing of the Work will be the sole responsibility of the Publisher.

COPYRIGHT

The Publisher agrees to copyright the Work in the name of the Author, and to take all necessary steps to protect the rights of the Author under national and international law.

ROYALTIES AND LICENCES

The Publisher shall pay to the Author or his duly authorized representatives, the following advances and royalties;

(a) A royalty of —— per cent (——%) of the retail price NSR thereof on all copies of the Work sold less returns.

(b) —— per cent (——%) of the proceeds of any licence granted to another Publisher to bring out a reprint edition of the Work.

(c) No royalties shall be payable of copies furnished to the Author or on copies for review, sample, or other similar purposes, or on copies destroyed.

AUTHOR'S COPIES

The Author shall be permitted to purchase copies for his/ her personal use at a discount of —— percent (——%) of the retail price.

LAW

This agreement shall be construed in accordance with the laws of the <Country of Publisher>.

INHERITANCE

This agreement shall be binding upon and inure to the benefit of the heirs, executors, administrators and assigns of the Author, and upon and to the successors and assigns of the Publisher.

ALTERATION

This agreement may not be modified, altered or changed except by an instrument in writing signed by the Author and the Publisher.

APPROVAL

Notwithstanding anything to the contrary herein contained, the Publisher shall obtain the Author's written advance approval of any jacket or cover design, including the text thereof, to be used in connection with the Work, and of any contracts with third parties for the publication of the Work; which approval shall not be unreasonably withheld.

AUTHOR...
WITNESS FOR THE AUTHOR...

PUBLISHER..
WITNESS FOR THE PUBLISHER.....................................

How digital markets change the author-publisher relationship

Books are published in hardback, trade and mass-market paperback editions; they are issued in special editions for international and special sales. Books are translated, issued as audiobooks, adapted for different media, and used as the basis for plays, films, games and other merchandise.

In its early days, the e-book was seen as just another format, a new subcategory that had to be added to the list of subsidiary rights covered by the contract. However, it soon became clear to agents, authors and publishers that the supply of intangible digital copies of a work (in the traditional volume form or as shorter parts) was going to involve the development of new contractual models and financial arrangements. There was a shift in the relationships between creators, publishers, supply chain members (including booksellers, libraries and computer companies involved in publishing), digital end-users and traditional readers.

Among issues that publishers must now consider are how digital rights are handled in existing contracts for p-books, and what additional agreements need to be made for existing works. Will the publisher have exclusive e-rights or will these be shared with, or wholly remain with the author? What are the royalty rates for e-books?

Since the development of digital publishing and e-books, many of the contract's terms have changed quite radically. Publishing contracts must now cover a variety of e-book and enhanced e-book rights, including extensions and adaptations in the form of games, merchandise and other applications for mobile phones and tablets.

Co-editions and translation rights

Publishing is both a local business that caters to the needs of national and regional audiences who have a common culture and language, and a global business, where publications are exported around the world in their original form, in new editions and through adaptations and translations aimed at specific international readers. In the digital environment, even the smallest publisher can have a global outreach, and a small Irish publisher can, in principle, reach an Irish market in the US almost as easily as a Boston publisher.

The subsidiary rights to publish translations, same-language reprints for particular territories, adaptations, digests and other special editions are often controlled by the same publisher and included in the author-publisher contract. In these cases, it is the job of the rights department to grant licences to other publishers and others who wish to exploit the work. The income is split according to an agreed percentage between the publisher and the author.

When an arrangement is made with other publishers to produce a variety of editions (most common with illustrated books for which economies of scale can be enjoyed in printing colour plates in one long run) the contracts for these co-editions are agreed prior to publication.

Clark's Publishing Agreements

Most UK publishers use *Clark's Publishing Agreements* as a guide when creating their contracts. This book is now in its eighth edition (2010), revised by Lynette Owen. (L. Owen, *Clark's Publishing Agreements: A Book of Precedents*)

BASICS

PHOTOGRAPHY

02

David Präkel

LIGHTING

n
light of a particular
quality or the equipment
that produces it

Ethical:
aware-
ness/
reflect-
ion/
debate

a
va
academia

4.3
Co-editions
Publishers of highly
illustrated books often
produce editions to sell
in their own country,
and then hope to sell
co-edition rights to
foreign publishers.
Lighting was first
published in English
and has also been
published in eight
other languages; see
overleaf for examples
of some of these.

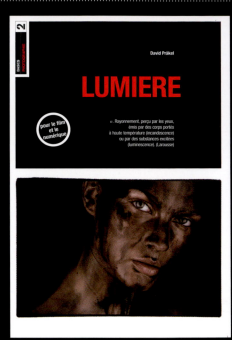

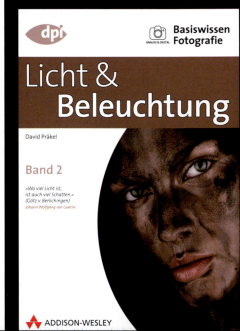

AVA BASICS PHOTOGRAPHY 2

데이비드 프래켈(David Präkel) 지음 | 김문호 옮김

4.4
Foreign editions
Different language editions will usually have covers that are geared to the needs and expectations of readers in their countries. Here we can see the covers of the Spanish, French, German and Korean editions of *Lighting* first published in English.

사진가를 위한
빛과 노출의 이해

세계적인 사진작가의 걸작을 통해 배우는 빛과 노출 그리고 조명 사용법!
로드 에드워즈, 에른스트 하스, 에릭 켈러만, 마리온 루이첸, 스콧 리트나워 외 다수

Discussion questions

1. What different editions might be covered by a publishing contract?

2. What commitments do publishers make in the contract?

3. What commitments do authors make in the contract?

4. What subsidiary rights might be sold by a publisher's rights department?

Editorial work: from submission to publication

After the commissioning or acquisition work is done, and the publishing proposal is developed sufficiently to form the basis of the author-publisher contract, another sort of editorial work begins. An editor will work with the author as he or she prepares the manuscript, reading drafts to make suggestions on style and content, ensuring that house style is followed, checking facts where necessary and encouraging the author to persevere at producing a text that will be fit for publication.

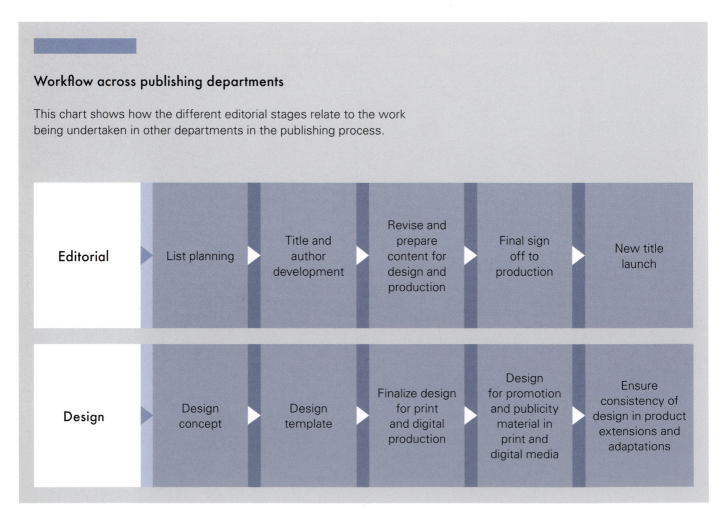

Workflow across publishing departments

This chart shows how the different editorial stages relate to the work being undertaken in other departments in the publishing process.

| Editorial | List planning | Title and author development | Revise and prepare content for design and production | Final sign off to production | New title launch |
| Design | Design concept | Design template | Finalize design for print and digital production | Design for promotion and publicity material in print and digital media | Ensure consistency of design in product extensions and adaptations |

Production	Estimates	Supplier quotations	Project manage – schedule and cost control	Coordinate print and digital production	Physical and digital publications delivered to supply channel
Sales and Marketing	Market research	Brand development	Detailed promotion and publicity plan	Manage communication and supply chain	New title launch
Contracts and Rights	Resource and legal implications	Approve contractual details	Subsidiary rights contracts agreed	Provide subsidiary licence holders with necessary materials	Ensure contractual compliance of company and partners
Finance	Financial planning	Approve investment	Monitor costs	Review costs and revenue projections	Review actual against planned financial performance
Management	Approve list proposal	Approve contract and investment in title	Monitor changes in budget	Monitor performance against plan	Assess success or failure

Developmental editing

Subject specialists and gifted writers benefit from working with knowledgeable and experienced editors, as do new writers and people used to writing in other media (such as newspapers, blogs, and academic papers). If the editor stays in constructive (but not too intrusive) dialogue with the author throughout the writing of a book, the author is far more likely to deliver a completed manuscript that fits the publisher's needs and expectations and to deliver the work on time and in an acceptable form. This is especially crucial for illustrated works, texts being developed for specific curriculum needs, and books when a team of authors are working on one book or series of books. At various stages the manuscript may also be sent out to others in the company, or to outside experts, for review and comment.

The file and the manuscript: copy-editing

When the digital file and/or physical copy of the manuscript are received, one of the first essential jobs to be done by the copy editor is to check that all the elements of the text and illustrations have been received and that these are all in the format agreed between the author and the publisher. The editor will also do a word count and estimate the extent of the finished book.

The editor will check that the text is organized in a consistent way, and that spelling and other elements of style such as punctuation are consistent and conform to the publisher's house style. (If there is a house style, then a guide to this will have been given to the author at the time the book was commissioned.) In addition to house style, standards like those in *The Chicago Manual of Style* (University Of Chicago Press) and *Butcher's Copy-editing: The Cambridge Handbook for Editors, Copy-editors and Proofreaders* (Cambridge University Press) may be used.

The marketing department will view this version of the text to develop the marketing messages, explore opportunities for collaborations with other parts of the supply chain and to develop the initial promotion of the book through websites and social media. Any questions that other departments may have about the book will be fed back to the author via the commissioning or acquisitions editor.

Checking the detail

The editorial work continues with a more detailed reading of the author's work, and this covers matters of style, grammar and spelling, and checks for clarity and accuracy. The editor queries passages that might appear ambiguous or obscure, and checks any facts in the author's text that might seem questionable. Some of the editor's changes are made directly to the file submitted by the author, while in other cases (especially where the text is written by a specialist) the editor asks the author for confirmation and/or clarification of any statement that might appear to be inaccurate, contradictory, illogical or illegal.

Employees and freelancers

Some publishers have quite large editorial departments with a full complement of commissioning editors, copy editors, production editors, and various other editorial assistants, but others have fewer members of permanent staff and rely on freelance workers such as proofreaders and indexers.

Giving an effective work brief to a freelancer is an important skill for the staff editor. All jobs must be accurately and fairly specified, and the time frame (the schedule and deadline for the work) and financial arrangements (the fee and when it is to be paid) agreed by both sides. The managing editor often oversees the work of outside contractors and freelancers.

Working with design and production

The editor marks up the manuscript with instructions for design and production. This ensures that the message of the book – and its appropriateness for the intended audience – is supported by the design and production values of the physical and digital product. It is important that the book's content and its form are complementary. (Chapter 5 explores design and production in more detail.)

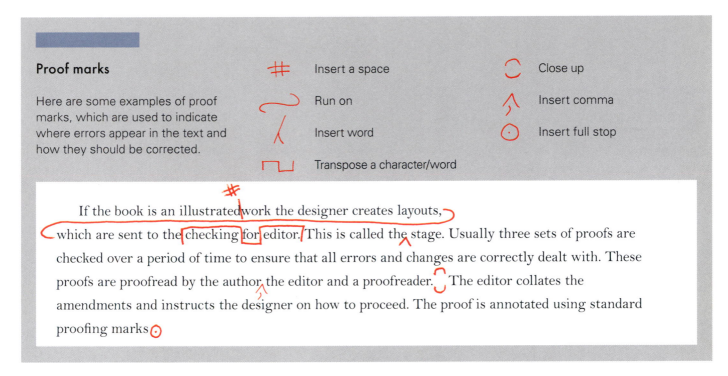

Proof marks

Here are some examples of proof marks, which are used to indicate where errors appear in the text and how they should be corrected.

#	Insert a space
	Run on
	Insert word
	Transpose a character/word
	Close up
	Insert comma
	Insert full stop

If the book is an illustrated work the designer creates layouts, which are sent to the checking for editor. This is called the stage. Usually three sets of proofs are checked over a period of time to ensure that all errors and changes are correctly dealt with. These proofs are proofread by the author the editor and a proofreader. The editor collates the amendments and instructs the designer on how to proceed. The proof is annotated using standard proofing marks

---

If the book is an illustrated work, the designer creates layouts, which are sent to the editor for checking. This is called the proofing stage. Usually three sets of proofs are checked over a period of time to ensure that all errors and changes are correctly dealt with. These proofs are read by the author, the editor and a proofreader. The editor collates the amendments and instructs the designer on how to proceed. The proof is annotated using standard proof marks (see above).

Working with marketing, publicity, sales and rights departments

Once the author has delivered the work, the price and publication date can be more accurately planned and the editorial and marketing departments can decide how the finished book can be finely tuned for the intended readership. In the time since the project was first discussed, there may have been developments in the subject area covered by the book; other publications may have appeared that offer competition to your book; and the priorities of the company's sales force and major partners in the supply chain may also have changed.

In the period running up to publication, editors keep in close communication with marketing, publicity and sales, as they agree on the cover design, promotional campaign, pricing and print-runs, e-book platforms, transmedia content, author promotional appearances and social media activities.

Editors also work closely with those selling other media and translation rights to ensure that they have suitable sample materials, author information and 'handles' to use when introducing the books to overseas publishers and other media producers.

Discussion questions

1. How do editors work with other members of the publishing team?

2. What qualities does a good editor need?

3. What is house style?

4. Who is involved in proofreading?

Case study:

A guide for

dummies

The *For Dummies*® brand (note the trademark) is an excellent example of how a publishing list can be developed for a global market. The series is now published by John Wiley & Sons, which acquired Hungry Minds (the new name for IDG Books as of 2000) in early 2001, although the brand *For Dummies* is always more prominent than that of Wiley.

The first title, *DOS for Dummies*, was published in November 1991 by IDG Books. The following titles in the series built on the success of the first title, being geared to show ordinary computer users how to make the most of their PCs, get on the Internet, and explore Windows. The editors in charge of the new list made an informed judgement that Windows would overtake DOS as the operating system of the masses. *Windows For Dummies* remains the bestselling computer book of all time.

The editorial intention is to produce books that are detailed but light-hearted. Aiming to make difficult material interesting and easy to understand, the books include cartoons and helpful lists.

The editors have kept on top of current trends, and recent titles have included *Flipping Houses For Dummies*, *Manga For Dummies*, *eBay For Dummies*, *Blogging For Dummies*, and *Food Allergies For Dummies*.

The series has developed into a list with a combination of solid backlist titles (over 250 million *For Dummies* books were printed up to 2011), and the ability to launch titles on up-to-the-minute trends, for example 200,000 copies of *GPS Navigation For Dummies* have been sold. The brand goes beyond print to include software, videos, and the Internet community.

International markets

There are more than 1,600 titles in English, and international editions are published in more than 30 languages worldwide including Arabic, Estonian, Greek, Russian, and Vietnamese. In many markets the English word 'dummies' is used as the brand, although in France the series is called *Pour Les Nuls*. Amazingly 600,000 copies of *L'Histoire de France Pour Les Nuls* have been sold, making it the bestselling foreign language title in the series.

Local editorial programmes produce titles for specific national markets, and the series includes a vast range of topics from computers to cooking, gardening to golf, soccer to sex, finances to flower arranging, travel, exercise, nutrition and mental health.

'In November 1991, *DOS For Dummies* by Dan Gookin was initially met with skepticism — most bookstore chains didn't want to carry the book at all, claiming that the title insulted their customers and readers in general. But we responded to the critics by calling the title a "term of endearment" that readers would immediately relate to and identify with. After convincing the bookstores to give us a chance, consumers agreed.'

The For Dummies *Success Story website*

4.5

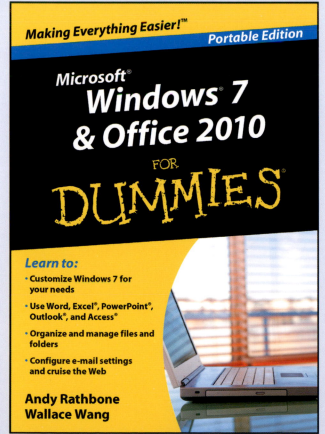

4.5
For Dummies
The *For Dummies* covers are distinctive and readily recognizable across a crowded bookshop, study or work station. They encourage readers to accept that they need help to understand and master a new skill, and the public has learnt that this series is a good way to get such help.

Key points

Creating a successful publishing list, and a globally recognized publishing brand like *For Dummies* requires a well-planned and executed commissioning strategy.

- When IDG first published *DOS For Dummies*, booksellers were reluctant to stock a book that appeared to denigrate the customer. The editorial judgement of the publisher proved to show a better understanding of the book buyer than that shown by the booksellers. The editorial approach, authorial tone and design elements formed the base of a memorable brand that is effective across very different subject areas.

- The yellow cover, the standardized typography and content design, and the consistent level of expert but accessible writing have all added to the trust that consumers have in the brand. While the design is a major visible clue to this approach to readers, it is the editorial style, and the editorial guidance given to authors, that determines the effectiveness of the way the information is presented.

- The first *For Dummies* titles were aimed at a new market group – people who needed a simple way to learn more about the software that was installed on their computers. Many other publishers jumped on the computer book bandwagon at the time, but *For Dummies* understood something important about their target market. The potential readers knew that they didn't know what they needed to know, and, so long as they got the information in an accessible and entertaining way, they were prepared to be referred to as 'dummies'.

- *For Dummies* have used the brand to provide other products and services. These include merchandizing of musical instruments, which started with the *Acoustic Guitar Starter Pack For Dummies* in 2006 (which packaged a guitar with a *For Dummies* book) and today includes a complete line of *For Dummies* instrument packs. In other brand collaborations the publisher produces custom packages, such as when a *For Dummies* team worked closely with Google to produce a print and online guide on using Google AdWords.

Activity

There are other series of books that compete with *For Dummies*. The *Teach Yourself* series was launched in 1938 and grew rapidly in response to wartime needs. It now includes over 500 titles, from Arabic and beekeeping to yoga and Zulu. The *Teach Yourself* imprint is part of the Hodder Education Group.

If you compare the *For Dummies* and *Teach Yourself* lists you may be able to identify evidence of different editorial approaches to what might appear to be very similar markets.

1. What subject areas have each of the companies chosen to specialize in when commissioning new titles for the publishing list?

2. Can you detect a difference of editorial approach in terms of how the readers are presented with a particular authorial voice and design style?

3. What can you find out about the different ways the two lists have developed digital enhancements or e-publishing formats?

4. What shows that these two lists are developed for an international market?

Design and production

Now that there are so many formats and digital platforms for publications, publishers have lots of new decisions to make. Will a guidebook be better as a printed book or as an app for an iPhone, iPad or other mobile devices? How can e-books be designed for all the different e-readers? What traditional print formats will be best for which markets? Can all the different versions be produced from the same data file? These are all things that require design and production skills, and the confidence and ability to manage publishing projects destined for a variety of formats for what might be widely different markets.

In all this, publishers need to be constantly aware of the importance of quality in the content and form of what they are producing. They need to be able to develop and keep to realistic schedules, budget effectively and establish pricing policies that lead to financial success. This chapter looks at how the design and production people in publishing contribute to this process and gives pointers on how to manage this important publishing function.

Platforms and formats appropriate for the content

The proliferation of formats and platforms for both print and digital publications requires managing content in a standardized way, so that it is possible to adapt this content for delivery to various markets through an array of production and distribution channels. An academic publisher, for example, can use the same core data files to prepare printed and online journals, printed books of conference papers and on-demand copies of individual articles. A trade publisher can use one file to create a hardback printed book, an e-book, and editions customized for other English-language markets. These editions may require new typefaces, formats, and designs, and even different spelling conventions. Content may be 'sliced and diced' into chapter length (or shorter) sections for delivery through mobile phones and other devices, allowing publishers, like other media companies, to become aggregators and editors of content from a wide variety of sources.

The foundation of published works

Digital files have mostly replaced paper manuscripts at the core of publishing. These may be simple word-processed documents, more complicated files containing hyperlinks, audio and video content, or transmedia creations with an even richer content. In this context, creating one file (in a format such as XML) makes the content useable across a wide variety of platforms and formats, and it can be efficiently transferred between publisher, designer, printer and e-book distributor.

Using a common file format makes it possible to allocate identifiers for digital rights management (DRM). The integrated development of metadata, including unique identifiers in addition to the ISBN, enables discrete parts of any publication (such as sections, chapters, illustrations, and appendices) to be identified and their usage tracked. Each file or sub-file can be identified by its DOI, the ownership of which can be validated and transacted across the global publishing network where others can create 'new' publications constructed of aggregated content.

Design decisions reinforce brand and access to the market

Designing even the simplest publication entails a number of critical decisions related to the format, typography, page layout, medium and packaging. These decisions involve a dialogue between the editor, designer and marketing manager, with regular reviews by senior management, to make sure that the content and presentation remain focused on the intended market. Whether the design is predetermined by the established style of an imprint or series, or whether it is a stand-alone, every decision affects the features and benefits that will influence readers (and everyone else in the publishing network) as they decide whether to buy, recommend, or read the publication.

Just as editors are usually guided and constrained by a 'house style', designers are likewise rarely given a blank canvas. Certain design and production features are dictated by industry norms such as standard book sizes (see page 122), limitations of printing technology, and customary prices for books and other publications. Each publisher decides on the design features and production qualities that it wants for a particular list or series. The standard features may extend to the choice of formats, typefaces, papers, bindings, and cover illustrations, so the challenge for the designer is to work within the constraints of the overall style to create readable, user-friendly and economical designs.

5.1

5.1
Brand and design
Design and production are now about much more than packaging one version of a publication. They are about brand, legacy, product integration and market penetration. Here you can see how a reproduction of one of the first covers of Agatha Christie's *The Body in the Library* is used as the design for a deckchair, extending the brand into an unexpected area of merchandizing.

A design brief

A design brief or memo for an individual title may include instructions on some of the following:

- The format of the book and overall page layout to be followed, including the body text area and the placing of different text elements such as running heads, page numbers, notes, and tables. The designer will generally be provided with (or will develop) a grid to ensure that these elements are consistent.

- Is the book to be in colour or black and white only, can it include spot colour or halftones? These decisions are made with marketing in mind, by consideration of the use of illustrations in competing titles, and by calculating the economic implications of the added cost of colour reproduction.

- Which typefaces (in what point sizes) are to be used for the various elements such as body text, captions, headings, and page numbers? This will be a part of the house style, and may well be built into the on-screen design template used by the designer.

- What illustrations are to be included? Is the designer expected to prepare illustrations or adapt those provided by the author, editor or picture researcher? These decisions are made by the editor and the author, but it is the designer's job to make sure that they are integrated appropriately into the overall publication as it will be experienced by the reader.

In the next chapter we'll look in more detail at the choices that relate specifically to the print versus digital decision, but first let's consider the publishing design decisions that confront publishers of print products.

Using InDesign

Adobe InDesign® is currently one of the most common software programs used by designers to produce files for books, magazines, newspapers, flyers, brochures, and other printed publications. InDesign files include page formatting information, page content, linked files, styles, and colours.

InDesign produces .indd files that are then converted to PDF files for use by the printer. Printers may use a variety of PDF file formats, depending on the different resolution required. The PDF file format, familiar to consumers from a multitude of Internet downloads, is also used for some e-books, although it does not offer all the functions available with other file formats.

Key design elements

This example of a spread shows some of the key design elements used in this book.

B-level heading

Introductory text

C-level heading

Body text

Navigation

Caption

Box

InDesign template

When a designer uses a design package such as InDesign (shown here), the design template will be determined before any actual content is included. Images may appear as blank pages, and text will often be substituted using *lorem ipsum*, a sample Latin dummy text that has been in use since the 1500s.

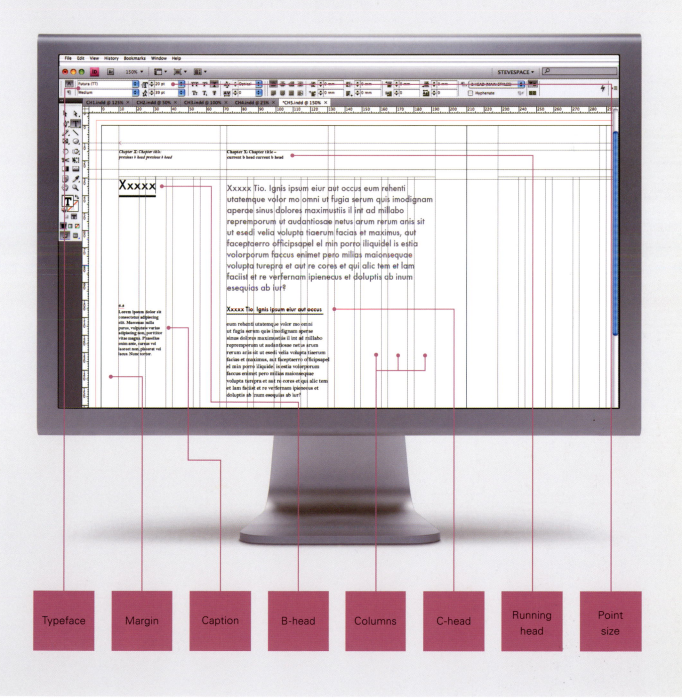

Typeface · Margin · Caption · B-head · Columns · C-head · Running head · Point size

Physical format

Printed books can come in all shapes and sizes, but the vast majority are produced in a small number of formats. Having standardized book formats means that printers can develop their production lines to offer cost savings, and production costs can also be controlled by using paper economically.

Slightly different book sizes (also called trim sizes) are used in the UK and the US, see below. Books produced in other parts of the world are printed on different sized paper, or are trimmed to formats that have a traditional place in their respective book markets.

Most books are produced in a portrait orientation, although some are landscape and some are square. Book production has become more global, with much production in recent years being done in China, India and other expanding economies. In this globalized publishing world, book formats are gradually becoming more standardized. This has rationalized many aspects of production and made life much easier for other parts of the distribution chain, from packaging to shelf display.

UK sizes	Metric (h x w) approx. trim size
Paperback sizes	
A format	178 x 110 mm
B format	198 x 129 mm
C format	216 x 138 mm
Other popular sizes	
Demy quarto	276 x 219 mm
Crown quarto	246 x 189 mm
Royal octavo	234 x 156 mm
Demy octavo	216 x 138 mm

US sizes	Imperial (w x h) approx. trim size
Mass-market paperback	4¼ inches x 7 inches
Paperback	5½ inches x 8½ inches
Common hardback sizes	6 inches x 9 inches 7 inches x 10 inches 8½ inches x 11 inches

Book formats

Book formats developed from the names of the sheets of paper used, and were traditionally named after the number of times a piece of paper was folded to make the size of the book. Thus the paper size called Crown (16 ¼ x 21 inches, 413 x 533 mm) leads to book sizes such as Crown Royal, Crown Quarto and Crown Octavo depending on the number of times the sheet is folded, and other paper sizes make different quarto and octavo sizes.

Modern book size names are still based on these measurements, although the metric size is the standard in the UK and the rest of the world, except in the US, where sizes are in inches, and expressed as width x height, rather than height x width.

"Producing a hardback edition gives publishers more flexibility", Baboneau said. "It's good to have the option of another edition up your sleeve; to do the hardback, and then be able to tweak the jacket and add quotes when you do the trade paperback edition and then the mass-market paperback. It means you can give a book that extra push." She added that, though there was little price differential between formats, "subconsciously publishers and agents love a hardback, and reviewers do too – it's something about the colour of the boards, the flaps, the feel of it for book buyers."

Simon & Schuster publishing director Suzanne Baboneau, The Bookseller, *2011*

Page design

The traditions and conventions of page design that have arisen over the years are based on the assumption that the design should make the text more legible; ensure that the organization of the work is clear to readers; and aid readers in navigating their way around the book. To help with navigation, a good design is internally consistent (according to house style), so that readers can quickly understand how the text and illustrations are organized.

Designers use various software packages to create pages for publication. Adobe InDesign and QuarkXPress are used by the majority of book designers although other major software suppliers such as Microsoft and Corel have similar design programs and some designers prefer to use open-source free software such as Scribus.

Designers need to have a good understanding of and training in issues of readability, the effect of design features on meaning, and how readers navigate around the physical page. Some e-books are unable to replicate all features of printed books when the content is moved into the e-book medium.

Typography

Typography – the choice of typeface, size and text layout – is a major factor affecting the readability of any text. Different typefaces are thought to be more appropriate to different types of publication. Most novels, for instance, are produced using a serif face such as Baskerville, Palatino or Times New Roman: they create links between letters so that the eye sees whole words, making prolonged reading easier on the eye and brain.

On the other hand, we have grown accustomed (through computer use and word-processed documents) to reading more factual work-related texts in sans serif typefaces such as Arial or Verdana. Scientists and academics used to PDF versions of documents, produced for publication in journals, are unlikely to experience anything other than a limited range of typefaces, while readers of fiction or poetry may be more used to the traditional serif characters.

The size of type is important. Large type is more easily read by children and those with limited eyesight. The point (pt) size determines how many characters there are in a line of printed text as it appears on the page or screen. The number of characters on a line of text can affect the readability, as can the kerning and tracking (spacing between letters), and the spacing (leading) inserted between lines. If our eyes have to move too often to the next line, or if they must move too far back to identify the start of the next line, reading is likely to be more tiring. Somewhere between 40 and 60 characters per line is a good measure. This preferred measure is also true of texts that are intended to be read on screen, so fixed-width pages for e-books can be far more readable than e-books in which the number of characters per line changes when the content is zoomed.

Different typefaces are used in the print culture of different countries, just as other design elements such as cover designs, formats, papers and bindings vary according to cultural traditions. The move to global digital publishing may have an effect on this creative diversity, as the tastes of publishers and readers become less bound by national and linguistic publishing traditions.

Typefaces used in this book

This book is set in:

Futura Medium

73pt

for chapter opener headings

20pt
for section headings

13 pt for section introductions

10 pt for sub-headings

Monotype Bell regular and **bold**

10 pt for main text

8 pt regular and bold
for the captions

Univers light and light italic
9 pt for box-outs and diagrams

Typefaces
The development of computer-based typesetting led to a growth in typefaces designed specifically for the new media.

Standard PC fonts	Some Macintosh fonts
Century Gothic	Avant Garde
Arial	Helvetica
Arial Narrow	Helvetica Narrow
Times New Roman	Times Roman
New Courier	Courier
Century Schoolbook	New Century Schoolbook
Bookman Old Style	**ITC Bookman**
Monotype Corsiva	*Zapf Chancery*

Typeface style
Type styles and weight are used for emphasis and differentiation

Non-Latin typefaces
Many non-Latin languages read top to bottom or right to left.

Typeface style		Non-Latin typefaces
Light	Helvetica Neue 45	**Chinese**
Roman	Helvetica Neue 55	诶 比 西 迪 伊 艾弗 吉 艾尺
Italic	Helvetica Neue 56	艾 杰 开 艾勒 艾马 艾娜 哦 屁
		吉吾 艾儿 艾丝 提 伊吾 维 豆
Condensed	Helvetica Neue 57	**Japanese**
Extended	Helvetica Neue 63	い/イ き/キ し/シ ち/チ に/ニ
Bold	Helvetica Neue 75	ひ/ヒ み/ミ り/リ ゐ/ヰ う/ウ
Black	Helvetica Neue 95	く/ク つ/ツ ぬ/ヌ ふ/フ む/ム

Illustrations

Illustrations are selected by an author, editor or picture researcher and can be an important part of the overall book package. A copy of the illustration required (usually in digital form) is obtained, and the cost and copyright clearance agreed. Some illustrations may need to be drawn (or redrawn) by a designer or artist. Expectations regarding the graphic quality of illustrations are developing to include HD and 3D images, and the text component of some transmedia publications may be much smaller than the other components as graphic elements gain prominence. With some multiform digital publications, the designer will have to make more complex decisions on the graphics and sound files that may become part of the overall transmedia package. When the content is 'reflowed' into the digital medium, images and text need to be linked together so that they appear in a useful juxtaposition.

Paper

Except for a very few books that are printed on plastics, fabrics or other exotic materials, most p-books are printed on paper, and their covers are printed on a paper board of some kind.

The choice of what paper to use is often quite simple, as all printers keep a stock that is suitable for the kind of books that they produce and it is usually sensible (and more cost-effective) to use the paper the printer has in stock. As the printer buys a lot of this paper, it should be reasonably priced, and of a quality already tried and tested on the machines to be used. The publisher only needs to buy the exact amount needed to print the required quantity, and the same stock is also likely to be available for any subsequent reprint.

Most books are printed on slightly off-white (to reduce the glare) or white paper. Book papers are light-weight (between 70 and 100 g/m²) and can have a range of bulk (thickness or calliper). In the US paper weight is calculated in pounds per ream (500 sheets). It is the bulk of the paper rather than the weight that determines how thick it is. Customers often compare the thickness of a book with its price, so the bulk can often be particularly important for the marketing of books with fewer pages.

The opacity of the paper is also important, and publishers are always concerned not to put off readers by using a paper that has too much show-through, particularly with pages that contain a mix of text and illustration. Bibles, however, are usually printed on 'Bible paper', which has low opacity, low weight and little bulk.

Knowledge of paper is like knowledge of fine wine; the connoisseur can describe many subtleties in glowing terms, while many others will just know what they like. Most publishers will play safe and choose a paper because it is available from their printer, it works with similar books, and it is available at a reasonable cost.

Paper production is resource-intensive and can cause pollution. It requires large volumes of water, energy and some chemicals as well as wood pulp. It is a major contributor to greenhouse gas emissions, being the third greatest industrial greenhouse gas emitter in the OECD (OECD Environmental Outlook). The Green Press Initiative and Forest Stewardship Council (FSC) and Sustainable Forestry Initiative (SFI) are just three of the programme that the publishing industry has adopted to improve on the environmental impact. Publishers with 'FSC Chain of Custody' certification include HarperCollins, Bloomsbury and Penguin, which produce most publications on FSC paper. SFI certified sourcing labels show that the fibre used to produce paper is from a legal and responsible source.

5.2

5.2
Colour photographs
Colour photographs
are reproduced using
techniques that apply
different inks (usually
magenta, yellow, cyan
and black) to produce
a full palette.

5.3
**Duotone
photographs**
Generally, duotone
photographs are used
for heightened visual
effect, and printed
in black and one
other colour.

5.3

5.4
**Black and white
photographs**
Black and white
half-tone photographs
are sometimes used for
their dramatic effect.
They are also usually
cheaper to print as
they use only one
colour of ink.

5.4

5.5

5.5
Line drawings
Line drawings have no
variation of ink
coverage, but rely on
the variation of
thickness of the lines
for effect.

Bindings and covers

Printed books come in a variety of bindings and covers. The choice of binding depends on the type of book and the market for which it is intended. Casebound or hardback books are usually produced for the top end of the market. Despite an increasingly uncertain market (according to the Association of American Publishers US hardback sales dropped by 25.4% in the 12 months from June 2010), they are back in fashion for trade books (both fiction and non-fiction), as publishers seek to differentiate print books from e-books by stressing their tangible and collectible qualities.

The pages of hardback books are often sewn in sections, as are those of some paperback books. Most paperback books, though, are assembled using burst binding (perfect binding), in which the signatures (pages in multiples of four, eight, 16 or 32) are held together by glue.

Hardback and paperback books usually have an illustrated jacket or cover printed with an image, typographic design, basic metadata (title, author, ISBN, barcode) and promotional material. This includes the promotional blurb, review quotes, endorsements and biographical information about the author, the major characters and any other important facts, such as series or film adaptations.

Cover designs attract attention, define genre, and create brand identity for imprints, authors, and series. For thrillers like the French *série noire*, romances like Mills and Boon/Harlequin, children's books like Ladybird, and the many Penguin sub-lists (Pelican, Modern Classics, Puffin), covers have long been a major component of book marketing. The design of the cover is thus of great importance to the publisher, the bookseller and the reader and represents an important part of the contribution designers make to publishing.

Most websites selling e-books feature a graphic identical or similar to the printed cover. For books published only as e-books, publishers recognize that there should be some visual clues about the genre and information on the text and the author. Given the nature of e-book purchases, this may include video material, interviews, readings, messaging services and interactive reviews. For the digital native generation, e-books sit comfortably alongside social network pages, SMS correspondence, and multiplayer games.

5.6

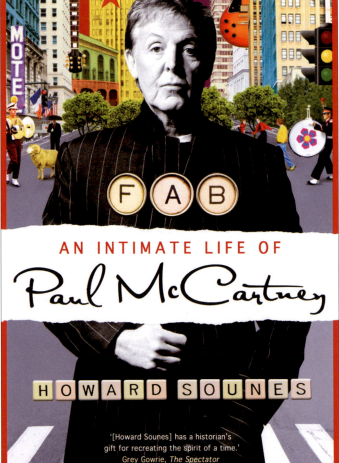

5.6
Covers
The covers for both the hardback and paperback of this book about Paul McCartney, published by HarperCollins, use the same graphic. It includes many elements from McCartney's life and work, which fans can enjoy piecing together and evokes the spirit of the sixties with which he is associated.

'What I as an author feel about this enormous change we're undergoing? It feels like I'm tied to the front of a runaway train where the driver's just had a heart attack, that's what it feels like.'

Philip Pullman, author of the His Dark Materials *series*
<www.digitalbookworld.com/2011>

Portability

One feature of the book remains constant: the e-reader fits, like the paperback book has done for many years, neatly in a bag or pocket. The fundamental portability of the book remains one of its most valued qualities; only now, as an e-reader, it can carry whole libraries.

Printing basics

The first printing presses made direct impressions onto paper or other media from inked blocks that carried raised type or pictogram characters. Printing by direct impression (letterpress) continued into the twentieth century, becoming increasingly automated and fitted to the requirements of mass production. The development of automated hot metal typesetting (to replace the hand assembly of cold type) during the 1880s (linotype) and 1890s (monotype), massively increased production capacity and improved the quality of reproduction. These innovations in typesetting, combined with the adoption of lithographic printing during the same period, provided the basis for the expansion of print publishing during the twentieth century. Central to this growth was offset lithography, in which the inked image is transferred (or 'offset') from a plate on a plate cylinder to a rubber blanket cylinder, from where it passes to the impression cylinder and then to the paper. Because there is no direct contact between the plate and the printing surface, this printing method produces a consistently high image quality and the plates have a longer printing life.

Modern offset presses can use paper in sheets (on a sheet-fed press) or in rolls (on a web-fed press). The efficiencies of continuous web printing make this especially useful for long runs such as those for newspapers, magazines, and mass-market paperback books. The modern printing press makes plates directly from data files. Digital technology allows the settings of the machine to be done automatically, which ensures accurate imposition and the correct flow of ink and paper for an individual job. Offset litho is still the cheapest method to produce high-quality printing in commercial quantities. Improvements in automated set-up now also make it appropriate for quite small print runs (in the low hundreds).

Digital printing is appropriate for small print runs of colour illustrated books. It is also employed by book printers who use POD and short-run printing for other types of books. On-demand copies of publications can also be produced on a local basis – sometimes within a conventional bookstore using, for instance, the Espresso Book Machine.

The number of pages in a book are multiples of the pages in a signature, for example a book composed of eight signatures each comprising 16 pages will have 128 pages. A signature is an individual section of a book made from a single sheet of paper folded in half, quarters, eigths and so on and then cut. A signature will usually consist of 8, 16 or 32 pages, although some presses can go as high as 64 or 128 pages printed on a single sheet.

Each book is designed in such a way that there is a minimum of blank pages on each signature, as this represents an unnecessary paper cost. The signatures are folded, and gathered together to form a book block, which is then bound together, covered and packaged. The first copies to come off the production line are inspected by the printer and the publisher's production department before being released into the supply chain.

5.7

5.7
POD books from a Xerox machine
Print-on-demand books like these can be made in a variety of formats, and can be trimmed to smaller sizes as required by the publisher.

5.8

Discussion questions

1. How is digital publishing affecting cover design?

2. What advantages are there to using standardized book formats?

3. When you read a novel, which typeface and type size do you prefer to read? Is this the same type style that you use on a computer screen?

4. What is the difference between sewn and perfect binding?

5.8
Colour proofs
Checking the quality of colour reproductions is an important part of production control. Here the operator is using a special magnifying glass, called a lupe, to get a close look at the way in which the different coloured inks have been applied to the proof.

Scheduling the publication process

One of the major determinants of the publishing production process is the time it takes to develop the final physical or digital product or service, so that it can be brought to market on a planned date. Production departments construct the production schedule backwards from the publication date decided by the publisher, taking all the various milestones into account. The design and production schedule dovetails with the editorial schedule, and runs concurrently with the marketing, promotion, sales and distribution schedule (see 'Workflow across publishing departments', page 108). All the elements must work together to give the publication its best chance in the market.

Time

It is the production controller's job to oversee the design and production activities undertaken both within the company and by external freelancers and commercial suppliers. The production controller needs to ensure that everyone keeps to the schedule, so that finished books are available for distribution in time for the publication date. At the same time, maintaining the schedule must not have a negative effect on quality. It is important to follow the schedule while keeping costs within agreed budgets and according to agreements with suppliers.

An effective workflow procedure means that spin-offs, repurposed versions, rapid revisions and adaptations to new platforms can be done in a cost-efficient way. Many publishers now use software technology to help with their workflow procedures, for example XML might be used to mark up text for e-publication. Many of the tasks done by copy editors, proofreaders, designers and web developers are now part of a common workflow that can ensure the simultaneous release of print, e-book, enhanced e-book or app. The use of XML means that the same content can be adapted for all these formats.

Project management

The fundamentals of production management remain as they were before the digital era: controlling the three variables of time, cost and quality. In other words, publishing on schedule, to budget and to the required specifications.

Digital workflow

The development of a digital workflow is seen by some as reflecting a fundamental shift in the publishing business model and the need for new publishing skills. Perhaps the most significant development is the need for a much closer working relationship between editorial and production, and this often entails a more integrated approach to new title development.

Content creation

Author creates content and/or publisher acquires rights to content.

Publisher ensures core content is suitable for delivery to different publishing audiences.

Conversion

Editor and designer adapt content to reader-orientated versions.

Format content for production in appropriate formats.

Publication

Design and production of content in different formats for different audiences (e.g. p-books, e-books, web pages).

Add appropriate metadata.

Delivery

Delivery of physical end-product (p-books) via bookstores and Internet booksellers or digital distribution (web, e-book, application).

Gather metrics via metadata.

Scheduling tools

As mentioned earlier, production schedules are generally created backwards from a date when copies are needed for distribution and launch into the market. Although computer-based scheduling has mostly replaced the use of wall charts, a good production coordinator will still need an instinctive feel for a likely delay before it happens and will quickly change his or her focus to react to possible critical points. All schedules are likely to be revised at points throughout the publication process, and the possibility of delays (known as 'slippage') must be built into any schedule.

Anyone buying production services from outside suppliers must be aware of the seasonal demand for these services. Getting a book printed in time for Christmas would need an October publication date and may be more costly and require tighter scheduling than at other times. Conversely, if publishers can print a publication at a time when there is not much other work on offer, they may be able to get a good price and very flexible service from printers.

The importance of quality

For most users, a well-produced book simply means accurate and entertaining content that is well written, well edited, and well produced. It must be easily navigable, with good quality production, so that the e-books work and the p-books don't fall apart. The layout, typeface and any graphics must work within an overall publishing concept like the *For Dummies* series (see the case study in Chapter 4). In the case of e-publications, the book must work at least on all the most popular devices from day one – something that may involve extensive trialling if there is a multimedia element to the overall product design.

The design must be appropriate to the reader's expectations and needs, but not overly sophisticated, unless enhanced features really add something to the user experience. The quality of e-books is about more than technical compatibility and marketability of e-books on different devices; and fundamental design qualities need as much care as with a p-book. Readers may excuse some spelling and grammar mistakes on e-mails and tweets, but they don't expect them in a book or an e-book. Copy-editing and proofreading remain a fundamental part of publishing in the digital age.

Proofs

The production process is punctuated by the different proof stages a book reaches in the process of typesetting, page layout and preparation for printing. Typeset material was traditionally first looked at in long galley proofs (unpaged impressions taken from the metal type put together by the typesetter), then in page proofs. First proofs are still corrected by the editor, author and designer, and changes made by each are incorporated into the finished work under the editor's control. When the page layout is finalized and images prepared for reproduction, proofs of illustrations show up any loss of clarity or colour definition, particularly in half-tone and colour illustrations. Further proofs are taken from the press before the final print-run, to check that imposition and colour values on the actual paper stock used in the printing are of the required quality.

Now that designers make up finished pages on screen, there are far fewer occasions when proofs are printed, and pages are often checked on screen with corrections made directly onto the digital file. This change to production methods does not mean that there is less need for meticulous attention to detail, and many editors and proofreaders still prefer to work with hard copy proofs that more directly mirror the physical book that will eventually be produced.

All of this proof checking is vital because the cost of paper and printing (the time the job takes on the printing press) are the most expensive parts of the production process for print publications. Because errors cannot be corrected once printing starts, proofs are often approved and signed off by senior staff.

The quality of the pre-press work is monitored using a proof that is either a soft (on screen) or hard copy (on paper) of what the final product will look like when it comes off the press. Hard copy proofing usually involves a high quality one-off copy of the production artwork, while soft proofing usually involves high-resolution computer images.

Digital production systems ensure that the text and images are produced accurately and consistently and can embed any coding necessary for the efficient delivery of the text in other formats and on other platforms. Thus the file used for storage, reproduction and distribution is provided with the metadata needed for it to be located, identified, and retrieved so that ownership, licensing, payment and attribution requirements are built into the structure of the publicly available (published) item.

What kind of reader?

Design is integral to the market expectations and aspirations that the publisher has for a particular publication, and the production department is involved from a very early stage in developing the product strategy. The published package is designed and produced with specific readers in mind, and takes into account the way in which these readers will use and enjoy it.

There is no doubt that reading habits are changing. Users of computers and mobile devices have become less used to deep or immersive reading (concentrated linear reading of one text at a time), and the ways in which content is presented (shorter texts, more graphics, stickier content) are changing to reflect this. Publishers are reacting to these developments in consumer behaviour in the same way that they have always paid attention to issues of readability and accessibility.

Discussion questions

1. Why is it important to construct the production schedule backwards rather than forwards?

2. Which is the most important element to control in the production process – quality, time or cost?

3. How might another department (not production) adversely affect the publications schedule?

4. What checks are made to ensure quality in the final published product?

Controlling costs and establishing prices

Whatever technology is used in the design and production of a publication, the responsibilities of the people who manage this part of the publishing process include the accurate estimation of costs prior to 'green-light' approval of the project; obtaining competitive estimates from appropriate outside suppliers and purchasing of services from the suppliers offering the best value and schedule for the service required; and the monitoring and control of costs throughout. This is done by maintaining good internal communications; working closely to understand the capabilities and limitations of suppliers; and having an effective system to plan and monitor expenditure.

Selecting suppliers

Production managers need to keep in close touch with their suppliers to maintain a good understanding of their capabilities. They must understand which printers are best for particular jobs, and also how to balance the requirements for quality with the need to get jobs done at an acceptable price and according to schedule. Developing mutual trust is important. Printers and other suppliers will make better deals with publishers who keep to deadlines, and provide all the required files and/ or other materials in agreed formats. Likewise, publishers prefer to deal with suppliers who keep to the schedule, follow the job specifications, and are transparent about how their charges are calculated. Most larger companies have lists of approved suppliers, which are subject to regular monitoring.

Estimates, quotations, contingencies and final costs

As we saw in Chapter 4, the production department provides a production estimate to the editor so that he or she can calculate the financial viability of the project in the form of a profit and loss (P&L) projection for approval by the management team. This estimate is made on the basis of their knowledge and experience, but when the publication is submitted by the author, the editor has better information about the details of the book (for example, its extent, number and kind of illustrations, any other special requirements) and the production department can obtain more precise quotations directly from suppliers. The production department may allow a certain percentage cost overrun for contingencies, but if changes are made to the specifications, revised quotations will be requested.

As the book progresses through the design, pre-press and production stages, the production controller will monitor progress and liaise with the editor and other departments to ensure that the schedule, quality and costs are in line with expectations. The production scenario may include a variety of outputs being launched simultaneously. This may require the coordination of the print and web design, the litho printing and digital file preparation, testing online and e-book delivery.

In some companies the production department has responsibility for processing and storing all the elements of the publication, so that they can be deconstructed and reconstructed in any way required by the complex supply and communications network that connects the publisher with its readers. Every production job is examined on completion to see if any cost, quality or scheduling elements might be improved through better management.

Pre-press and manufacturing costs

Publishing, like all manufacturing industries, has two major kinds of costs associated with producing the goods it sells. First, there are the costs of developing a project. These costs include paying for the creation of intellectual property (the text and illustrations), developing the design prototype (the production file), and the tools necessary to mass produce the product (printing plates). These one-off pre-press costs (sometimes called fixed costs or plant costs) are all incurred before the printing and binding, and are the same whether one copy or 10,000 copies are produced.

The costs of manufacturing, on the other hand, are related to the number of copies being produced once the press is rolling. While there are some economies of scale as more copies are produced (and the initial cost of setting up the machine is absorbed over more copies), the manufacturing costs (machine time, paper, ink, folding, binding and covering) are generally in proportion to the number of copies being produced. A lot of production, both pre-press and manufacturing, is done in emerging market countries, so freight costs, quality control via the Internet, and currency exchange rate variations must be taken into account and managed.

5.9
Printing

During the high-speed printing process, the different colour elements must be printed in exactly the right place on the sheet. If they are not, the colour printing is said to be 'out of register' and the results will be unuseable.

5.9

With digital production, the economic model of pre-press and manufacturing costs no longer applies. This is because when an item is delivered through digital platforms, the only production costs are really the product development costs and equivalent to pre-press costs for p-books. However, because of the technology involved and specialist skills required, these can be much higher than for a printed book. There are also additional costs involved in distributing and marketing e-books, such as the need to ensure proper adherence to EPUB® standards. The commonly held idea (by a broad group from writers to book buyers) that e-books are cheap to make is an illusion that has been reinforced by the loss-leader promotions that some device manufacturers have made in order to increase profitable sales of e-reading devices.

Discussion questions

1. Why do the economics of physical publishing production favour larger print runs?

2. What is included in pre-press costs?

3. Why might one printer be better than another for a specific job?

4. Why do publishers prefer some suppliers over others?

Case study:
Horrible Histories

Horrible Histories show how content can be designed and packaged for specific audiences. There is a series of books, published by Scholastic in the UK, a TV series and game show. Terry Deary, who writes the books, is one of the UK's best-known authors of children's books.

The books are designed to interest younger children in history by concentrating on unusual and gory historical tales. Since the publication of the first titles (*The Terrible Tudors* and *The Awesome Egyptians*) in 1993, there are now over 60 titles, which have sold more than 25 million copies in 30 languages. With the TV series, computer games, and other franchised spin-offs, *Horrible Histories* is now a major publishing brand.

The books are vividly designed, and include page layouts and typography that are more associated with comic books, newspapers and other printed ephemera than traditional history books. They also have a considerable online presence and a range of audiobooks and e-books.

In 2011, Scholastic announced a number of significant developments to the *Horrible Histories* brand, in particular by developing Internet portals that can enable visitors to explore all aspects of the series, and participate in quizzes and games.

- The *Gory Games World* Internet portal was launched in 2012 in time for the Olympic Games in the UK. The company has tied it in with a TV programme, *Horrible Histories: Gory Games*, co-hosted by Rattus Rattus, in which three horrible historians test their knowledge of the beastly bits of history with quirky quizzes, gory games and grisly prizes.

- It has developed an Internet portal for *Horrible Science*. The *Horrible Science* series has partnered with Galt Toys to offer *Horrible Science* experiment kits, that encourage children to concoct slimy materials, construct rockets, and make model eyeballs.

- The *Horrible Histories* books are available as e-books for Kindle.

- The 'HorribleHistoriesWorld.com' is being developed as a revenue earner, with subscriptions and virtual world purchases, using online currency 'groats', as well as click-through advertising. Subscribers will get a 'room that they can customize', such as an Egyptian tomb or a pirate cabin, and will also be able to use virtual currency, and access games, quizzes and quests.

- At the time of the launch, Steve Richards, head of the firm developing the website, said: 'Any brand moving in the virtual world needs to be distinctive and to be spread across a number of areas such as television, books and film or sport.'

- People placing orders with Scholastic in the UK (the publishers of *Horrible Histories*) can nominate a school or charity to receive 20 pence for every £1 that is spent. This is good for business, and good for the reputation of the publisher.

5.10

5.10
Horrible Histories website
The website connects viewers to the wonderful world of *Horrible Histories*, a virtual world that can be explored, where books can be bought and much more.

5.10
5.11

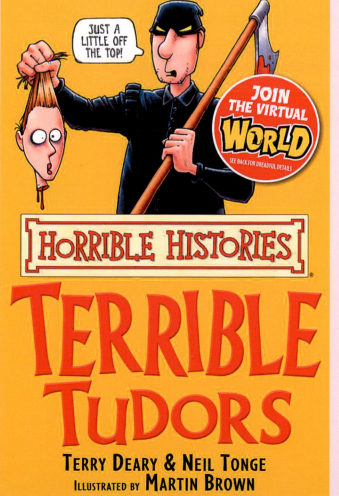

5.11
Terrible Tudors cover
One of the things that appeals to the young readers of *Horrible Histories* is the mix of humour and the macabre reflected in this cover.

Key points

The design for a series like *Horrible Histories* is developed with an eye to the publisher's perception of the target market, so it is worth testing design elements with potential readers. The design must also be adaptable for different print and digital formats and be useable for co-editions and international editions.

- **Designing for an age group:** *Horrible Histories* are not produced for the school curriculum, so there are no constraints to design for a particular age group. Children from six to 16 can enjoy them, as do many adults.

- **Design elements for e-books:** As the design style is such a strong feature of the brand, Scholastic decided not to do an early launch of *Horrible Histories* as e-books, preferring to wait until issues related to copy flow and illustration were resolved.

- **International production:** Like Dorling Kindersley titles in a previous decade, *Horrible Histories* are ideal for co-publication and adaptation for different market editions. In addition to rights licences for particular titles, overseas publishers have been encouraged to use the format concept to develop their own titles in the *Horrible Histories* style. This is a business model similar to TV franchising of popular show formats.

- **Transatlantic:** Scholastic publishes the *Horrible Histories* series in the US, and also publishes another similar series called *You Wouldn't Want to Be . . .* such as *You Wouldn't Want to Be a Chicago Gangster!: Some Dangerous Characters You'd Better Avoid.* This is an example of branding and associated design elements being adapted to local markets.

- **Brand protection:** *Horrible Histories*® is a registered trademark. While titles and series titles are not protected by copyright law, some are protected by the much stronger designation of trademarks. In another famous example, Frederick Warne & Co owns the trademark rights of the Beatrix Potter characters.

- **Social network:** The *Horrible Histories* portal is being launched on subscription. Could this be a model for future publisher websites, emulating some of the web developments in newspaper and magazine publishing?

Activity

Find out about the international publishers involved in the *Horrible Histories* series and compare their titles, design elements and promotional messages. Compare these with other children's publishing.

1. What are the common design and production elements in the different editions?

2. To what extent is *Horrible Histories* designed as a global brand?

3. To what extent has the *Horrible Histories* publishing formula been applied differently in response to local market conditions by publishers around the world? How does the design of the original series help to facilitate the production of international adaptations?

4. Look at the websites of a variety of children's publishers and compare the design used. What other membership, subscription or social network models can you identify?

5. Do you think it is right to treat a potentially serious subject like history in such a light-hearted way and to use such bright and playful design elements?

Chapter 6

Print and electronic publishing

As the market for e-books continues to grow, authors, agents, publishers and booksellers make choices between a variety of media, formats and platforms. Within a technical, legal and administrative framework that sometimes struggles to keep up, new business models for both print and electronic publishing have been proposed. This chapter looks at some of the ways digital workflow and software standards are easing the smooth adoption of digital publishing for many types of publishing in local and global markets.

Business models for print and digital publishing now reflect changes in the marketing communication and supply chains, and make increased use of sales and distribution models that include a variety of new media channels.

Choosing from a variety of media and formats

6.1

6.1
Tablet
Many readers have become used to having a large number of titles in their portable library of e-books, available by a simple touch of the screen.

Readers have long been accustomed to the idea that books come in a variety of formats and bindings, with varying production qualities in terms of design, typography, printing techniques and paper. When publishers first started to make texts available in digital formats the digital rights were seen as a further subsidiary right and the printed book remained the basis of 'volume rights' that is the rights to publish the book in printed form. With the rapid growth of e-books and an increasing array of tablets and other digital delivery devices, publishers now have many more ways to publish, and the printed work no longer has an unrivalled position in publishing.

Moving from print to digital

A growing number of consumers now expect a variety of delivery mechanisms and increased media convergence, and publishers must understand how their publishing programmes will be consumed in different formats by different audiences.

Some types of publishing, particularly reference and journal publishing, have moved almost exclusively to digital publication. For other types of publishing, the shift is much more gradual.

Moving through different formats

New publishing media have developed in the last decade with the introduction of new formats that can be read on tablets and e-readers.

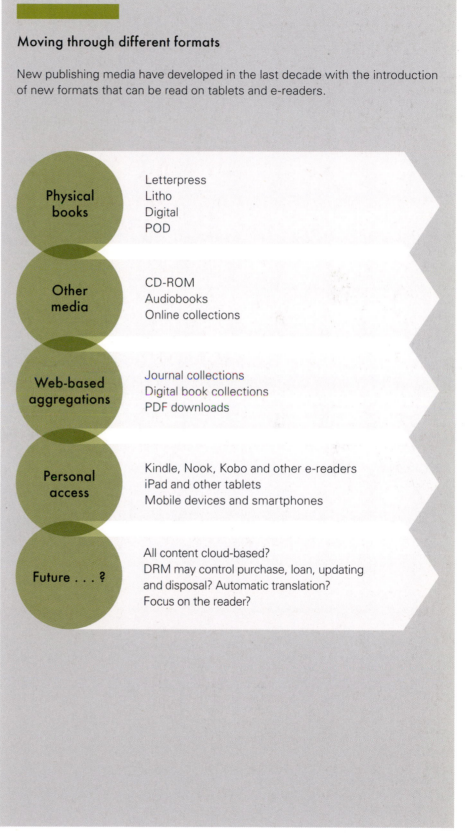

Physical books
Letterpress
Litho
Digital
POD

Other media
CD-ROM
Audiobooks
Online collections

Web-based aggregations
Journal collections
Digital book collections
PDF downloads

Personal access
Kindle, Nook, Kobo and other e-readers
iPad and other tablets
Mobile devices and smartphones

Future . . . ?
All content cloud-based?
DRM may control purchase, loan, updating and disposal? Automatic translation?
Focus on the reader?

Changing reading habits

The act of reading is changing. It is becoming both more private (we buy and consume e-books in a more anonymous way than we do with a physical book), and more public (we engage with other readers through reading groups, literary festivals, social media, publisher and author forums). Our digital libraries are not on display to visitors, but stored on our personal device or in our personal cloud space.

Advances in e-book technology aim to make the e-book reading experience (including the hypertextuality that often leads us away from the central text through our ability to click on live links) the preferred way of absorbing text. Readers can annotate e-books (just as they can use a pencil to make marginal notes in a paper edition), and use hypertext links to read more than the book. The 2011 success of Faber's digital *The Waste Land* (the iPad app covered its costs in just six weeks according to the *Guardian*, 8 August 2011) shows that there is a public appetite for such digitally enhanced texts, even of quite esoteric kinds.

The development of e-ink, back-lit screens and other ways of making the screen an acceptable replacement for paper are likely to ensure that e-readers become a major way in which much fiction and popular non-fiction is read over the next five to ten years. Other text-related features like search and annotation make the e-reader not only suitable for simpler narrative and instructional texts, but also for educational and academic materials.

Some elements of illustrated book design are more difficult to replicate in the digital environment, due to the reflowing of text and images (meaning that the original layout is lost). As technology develops to enable enhanced illustrations in e-books, richer graphic content is adding to the reading experience. A further significant e-book technological development is in the realm of interactivity, intermedia, hyperlinking and embedding of audio, video and other non-text materials.

Digital publishing developments also lead to the possibility of new forms of literary texts – poetry, stories and other narratives that are created in digital forms rather than being produced from static texts adapted for digital delivery. An early example of such a development was Papercut, an enhanced reading experience for iPad that included three short stories by Richard Beard, Nadifa Mohamed and Laura Dockrill, and provided what was described as 'an interactive, multi-sensory reading experience, automatically triggering relevant video, animation, image sequences and sound content'. Many other such publications have appeared in recent years.

6.2

6.2
The Waste Land
In adapting *The Waste Land* by T.S. Eliot as an app, Faber and Faber were able to add on other elements. These included interactive notes, a filmed performance and audio readings of the poem. For example, world-renowned Irish poet Seamus Heaney, above, offers perspectives on the poem.

'Technological change is discontinuous. The monks in their scriptoria did not invent the printing press, horse breeders did not invent the motorcar, and the music industry did not invent the iPod or launch iTunes. Early in the new century book publishers, confined within their history and outflanked by unencumbered digital innovators, missed yet another critical opportunity, seized once again by Amazon, this time to build their own universal digital catalog, serving e-book users directly and on their own terms while collecting the names, e-mail addresses, and preferences of their customers. This strategic error will have large consequences.'

Jason Epstein in his review of Merchants of Culture *by John B. Thompson (Polity) in the* New York Review of Books, *2011*

'Our digital program does not reside in a separate 'new media department' but is spread across the entire Press – Information Technology, Intellectual Property, Design/Production, Editorial, Sales/ Marketing, and Operations. Everyone owns digital; everyone has a professional stake in its success.'

Susan Wallace Boehmer, 'E-Tomorrow at Harvard University Press', Logos, 2011

Enhancing texts with ancillary material has been one reason for an increase in the price of many core text packages. Publishers can charge high prices when they have a relatively captive market, and try to recoup losses suffered because overall sales have dropped due to the increased use of second-hand texts. Publishers need to be aware that special features required in some disciplines (mathematical notations, chemical symbols, alphabets) may need special tools. The software used for digital works must also ensure that the copy flow keeps illustrations and tables close to relevant text.

Textbook formats

Textbook publishers produce supplementary materials to accompany their publications, including teachers' notes, self-test questions, and revision guides. These add-on learning materials (and the core text) are now often published in digital form, usually accessed online, sometimes free and sometimes for a price. They can include reference guides and glossaries, case studies, data spreadsheets, podcast audio and video lectures, and laboratory demonstrations. Publishers have moved quickly to adopt a variety of digital delivery channels for such material; from distribution via central university computer systems, to downloading to personal computers, tablets and other mobile devices.

Textbook databases also enable course tutors to customize text packages to include not only content from the original publisher, but also the tutor's own notes, presentations and lectures. They can also include material from other content providers like news media, specific company case studies, local regulations and other educational material. Digital publication also makes it easier to update texts, and to adapt content for local market conditions.

Another possible consequence of the ability of educational institutions or individual tutors to mix and match the content of a textbook is that the content can be changed to conform to an ideological, political or religious viewpoint. Digital texts – for example, books about history and evolution – could be more easily manipulated to put forward a particular point of view.

Trade book formats

In some trade categories (particularly in the US) e-books have overtaken print books (both hardback and paperback) in terms of unit sales (source: the *Guardian*, April, 2011). Many of the print sales and e-book sales go through the same channel (Amazon) and this has caused some concern about the future diversity of distribution channels.

In non-English language markets, countries where fixed book prices are enforced, and other markets with a strong independent bookselling tradition, e-book uptake has not been so rapid, but it is accelerating.

In poorer countries it will obviously be some time before the e-reading devices become affordable to a wide public, but the BRIC (Brazil, Russia, India and China) countries are moving to adopt mass usage of e-books, as are other markets in Asia, Latin America and Africa. The developments are rapid and are likely to continue to be so, making it difficult to predict or anticipate new shift.

However, it is clear that the scope, scale and momentum of digital developments will vary for different types of publishing. While fiction and non-illustrated non-fiction have made very rapid progression to e-book, other genres are proving more problematic. One book category that initially presented difficulties in transforming from print to e-book was the illustrated cookery book, and not only because people didn't want to spill soup on their iPads. For example, when the first attempts were made to convert Julia Child's classic *Mastering the Art of French Cooking*, there were issues about how to present lists of ingredients on the e-reader screen, how to preserve the two-column format already familiar to readers of this kitchen classic, and how to present the well-known illustrations. The publisher, Knopf (part of Random House), therefore waited until 2011 to publish the e-book version. This required its production staff to retype the whole book by hand, redesign the book from scratch, and add useful links. Even then some features, such as its distinctive typeface, which was familiar to the p-book readers, have been lost. Publishers and readers may keep a preference for printed cookery books, art books and other highly illustrated and annotated books for some years yet.

6.3

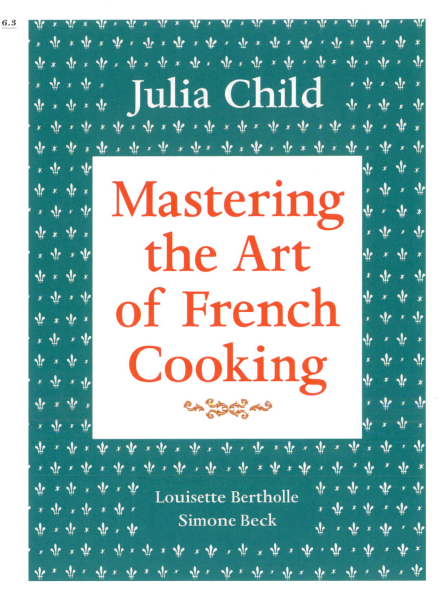

6.3
Julia Child
Mastering the Art of French Cooking (published by Random House) is a classic cookery book that is now available in e-book format. Cookery books remain a mainstay of the gift book market and most users continue to be loyal to the printed text when using a recipe book in the kitchen.

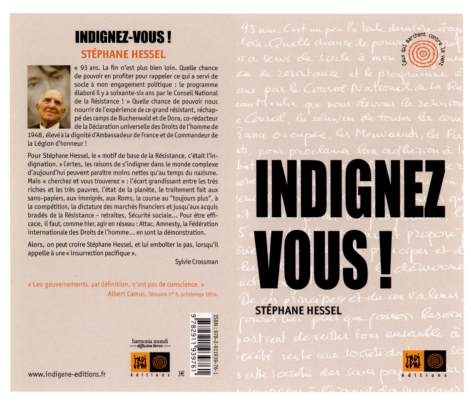

INDIGNEZ-VOUS !
STÉPHANE HESSEL

« 93 ans. La fin n'est plus bien loin. Quelle chance de pouvoir en profiter pour rappeler ce qui a servi de socle à mon engagement politique : le programme élaboré il y a soixante-six ans par le Conseil National de la Résistance ! » Quelle chance de pouvoir nous nourrir de l'expérience de ce grand résistant, réchappé des camps de Buchenwald et de Dora, co-rédacteur de la Déclaration universelle des Droits de l'homme de 1948, élevé à la dignité d'Ambassadeur de France et de Commandeur de la Légion d'honneur !

Pour Stéphane Hessel, le « motif de base de la Résistance, c'était l'indignation. » Certes, les raisons de s'indigner dans le monde complexe d'aujourd'hui peuvent paraître moins nettes qu'au temps du nazisme. Mais « cherchez et vous trouverez » : l'écart grandissant entre les très riches et les très pauvres, l'état de la planète, le traitement fait aux sans-papiers, aux immigrés, aux Roms, la course au "toujours plus", à la compétition, la dictature des marchés financiers et jusqu'aux acquis bradés de la Résistance – retraites, Sécurité sociale... Pour être efficace, il faut, comme hier, agir en réseau : Attac, Amnesty, la Fédération internationale des Droits de l'homme... en sont la démonstration.

Alors, on peut croire Stéphane Hessel, et lui emboîter le pas, lorsqu'il appelle à une « insurrection pacifique ».

Sylvie Crossman

« Les gouvernements, par définition, n'ont pas de conscience. »
Albert Camus, Témoins n° 5, printemps 1954.

INDIGNEZ VOUS !
STÉPHANE HESSEL

harmonia mundi
diffusion livres

www.indigene-editions.fr   3€

indi gène éditions

ISBN : 978-2-911939-76-1

6.4
Indignez-Vous!
'Take a book of just 13 pages, written by a relatively obscure 93-year-old man, which contains no sex, no jokes, no fine writing and no startlingly original message. A publishing disaster? No, a publishing phenomenon.' (*Independent*, 3 January 2011)

6.4

How long is a book?

Recent years have seen an increased consumer taste for shorter publications as both p-books and e-books, fiction and non-fiction (Kindle Singles, Workman Shorts, TED books – Technology, Entertainment, Design). The short story, the essay and other short forms of writing have been given new life by the growth of commercial e-publishing.

After many years when it was very difficult for a fiction writer to persuade a publisher to produce a collection of short stories, the technology of e-publishing has made it possible for individuals and small groups to publish and market these kinds of fiction titles themselves. In response, some reviewing media such as Kirkus (discussed in Chapter 3, on page 85) are focusing on the many new writings emerging in this form.

The publication of short issue-based publications (what might previously have been thought of as pamphlets) has grown since 2010 with the success of such collections as TED books (tied into the global TED conference and podcast phenomenon) and books published by the *Huffington Post* and other newspapers. Many of these short books are compilations of press articles. *Fortune* magazine published such a compiled e-book about Apple's Steve Jobs after his death.

One of the publishing phenomena of 2010–11 was the global success of 93-year-old Stéphane Hessel's short political essay, *Indignez-Vous!* (*Time for Outrage!*), which became a bestseller across Europe. Published by a small French publisher Indigène éditions, it sold over a million copies and was published in more than 20 countries.

Publishing without restraint

Digital backlist programmes such as E-Reads are making a vast supply of e-content available for sale (mostly reissuing publications that would otherwise be unavailable or 'out of print'). Other publishers, such as Bloomsbury, have acquired rights of previously out-of-print titles or taken advantage of titles in the public domain to publish new collections of 'classic titles' as e-books, just as they have previously done for printed volumes. This echoes the way that music companies produced boxed sets of remastered recordings on CD, and the movie industry repackaged and enhanced its wares.

6.5

6.5
Kobo
The Kobo platform is available worldwide and is 'device-neutral', meaning that its applications work on all computers and portable devices.

Outside of the major English-language markets, the first international expansion of e-readers and e-books concentrated on making English-language books and branded readers available to consumers in non-English-language territories. During 2011 – 'the year of the e-book' as predicted by Nigel Newton of Bloomsbury – this expansion took on different forms. Kobo launched an e-book service in Germany with an initial 80,000 titles in the German language out of a total of 2.4 million e-books. It also developed free German-language apps for iPhone, iPad, iPod touch, Android, and PlayBook. The Kobo German launch was followed by e-book stores in Spain, France, Italy and the Netherlands. In the UK, Kobo partnered with WH Smith.

Other major companies also played their part in promoting e-reading. Amazon launched in Europe and also in China in partnership with China International Publishing Group (CIPG). Apple initially focused its iBookstore strategy in over 30 countries in North America and Europe. Barnes & Noble made Nook alliances with independent bookstore chains in other countries. In some countries, local publishers and booksellers have launched other devices (such as the Hugendubel e-book in Germany) to cater to the needs of the non-English-language market.

Discussion questions

1. Which types of publishing have benefited most from the growth of digital publishing?

2. Should publishers make a distinction between print and e-publishing in the way that they organize their companies?

3. Is e-publishing altering the way in which writers write and readers read?

4. Why might e-publishing be increasing the output of short texts?

Legalities of publishing in a wired world

As an industry that derives its income from the ability to control rights to intellectual property, publishing is rightly concerned when changes in the market environment threaten the established business models. The development of the digital economy has led to a review of international conventions and agreements, redrafting of national legislations, establishment of industry codes of practice and a great amount of soul-searching, debate and discussion in an attempt to maintain stability in the market during this period of flux.

Contractual implications

As we have seen earlier, publishing contracts specify what rights are being granted to the publisher by the creator of a work. They must cover all present and future possibilities including printed editions, digital and photographic processes used to produce paper editions (including print-on-demand), online and digital formats. Contracts must cover the entire work and parts of the work that may be reproduced separately – on paper, on digital storage, on screen, or as printable downloads. In addition to the traditional plethora of subsidiary rights, the contract also covers use by library networks, by teachers and coursework pack producers, print and online media extracts, and any other photographic or digital reproduction of the whole work, part of the work, or a new arrangement of the work. Contracts are certainly not getting any simpler.

The rights are summarized on the copyright page of the publication, in the terms and conditions of any online or downloadable version, and are now often managed and monitored by the DRM and DOI built into the publisher's content management software.

Copyright notice

This copyright notice appears at the front of this book, and clearly sets out the rights of the publisher.

6.6

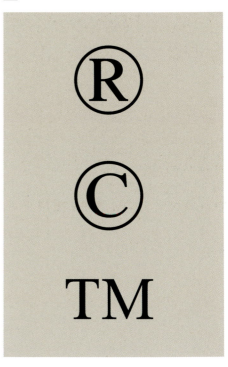

6.6
In addition to copyright ©, publishers can benefit from the common law protection that comes from using a trademark ™ (unregistered) or a registered trademark ®, which provides greater statutory protection.

Regulation in a borderless publishing environment

In spite of the efforts of multinational corporations and national governments to exercise territorial exclusivity, this is more difficult to regulate in the digital world, and there is a general move towards global rights and a reduction in the number of territorially restricted editions. When it comes to language rights, however, local publication is likely to remain the rule.

For local off-line printing, it may become more difficult to regulate local POD facilities without greater network security, and local printing of PDF files has created a consumer expectation of being able to print files downloaded directly from the Internet. The legal frameworks under which library systems operate will tend to be compliant with any DRM-based (digital rights management) monitoring system that is developed, and lessons about controlling access to digital resources learnt in academic libraries are being applied to the broader library world.

Cloud computing may also make the control of file transfer more difficult, and raises issues of accountability. The cloud accentuates issues about privacy and surveillance in the digital world.

Other legal considerations

As with all publications, digital communications and e-books run the risk of censorship. Views of obscenity and acceptable sexual behaviour can be enforced in the digital world, and political opinion can be monitored and taken out of circulation. Texts can also be subverted. It is far easier to alter a digital text than a physical one (particularly one held in the cloud rather than as a personal downloaded copy), and there are many examples of governments around the world blocking access to websites that they do not like.

While the underground printing press always stood the risk of being discovered, we should remember that printed *samizdat* publications (copies of banned or dissident literature) were still able to circulate in even the most repressive states. Will the same be true of digital messages now that governments have seen the power of social networks in spreading anti-government messages?

The author-publisher contract is always bound by the laws of a particular country, and the country of physical publication is significant in determining legal responsibilities; however, e-publications are generally available across national boundaries. In some instances (such as libel) this might mean that publishers may be liable under the laws of other countries. This is another example of the way in which digital culture has international implications.

Discussion questions

1. Which parts of the author-publisher contract have changed as a result of e-publishing?

2. How have traditional ideas about territorial rights been altered by the increase in digital publishing?

3. Does digital publishing lead to more freedom of expression and less censorship?

4. Should e-publishing be controlled by governments?

Digital workflow and software standards

The detailed process that transforms a creator's vision and textual output into a published work has increased in complexity now that the publisher must work with both print and digital media and distribution channels. The publisher may be required to develop a wide variety of products and services derived from the author's work, and a one-size-fits-all publication is no longer enough. In order to ensure a cost-effective process, most publishing now relies on the idea of having one reliable and adaptable core data file that can be used to generate any and all manifestations of a given publication – physical, digital, complete or fragmentary – that may be required.

Managing digital assets with .doc, .docx, XML and XHTML files

Most authors supply their text as a Microsoft Word (.doc or .docx) file to the publisher, with images, tables and other ancillary material supplied in the appropriate file formats, usually a TIFF, EPS or JPEG image file.

The publisher may convert the file to XML or XHTML, these are markup file languages that allow publishers to tag the various features in a book (such as images, captions, headings, and body text), making the designer's/typesetter's job easier and ensuring that they can be used for print and digital output.

XML files are readily used to store, transmit and output content for publication in many media and on different platforms. XML workflow enables the publisher, book designer, printer, website and e-book designer to adapt the file into the necessary formats.

EPUB3 and HTML5 for e-publishing

New methods of creating digital content mean that publishers need to switch their mindset from thinking first of print-based formats and tools. Increasingly, workflow management will enable them to develop their products and services across the whole range of media outputs. Markup languages, such as XML and XHTML can be used to produce varied enhanced e-publications in formats that conform to the specifications of EPUB3 standards.

EPUB3 (released in 2011) supports a wide range of publication requirements, including complex layouts, rich media, interactivity, and global typography features. It is utilized for a broad range of digital content, including books, magazines and educational, professional and scientific publications.

'As e-book sales mushroom, the Big Six's insistence on DRM has proven to be a hideous mistake. Rather than reducing piracy, it has locked customers in Amazon's walled garden, which in turn increases Amazon's leverage over publishers. And unlike pirated copies (which don't automatically represent lost sales) Amazon is a direct revenue threat because Amazon have no qualms about squeezing their suppliers – or trying to poach authors for their "direct" publishing channel by offering initially favourable terms.

Cory Doctorow, Stross: publishers' insistence on DRM 'hands Amazon a stick with which to beat them'

HTML5, a development of the HTML markup language that has been at the core of most web pages since the 1990s, has numerous new features designed to make it easy to include and handle multimedia and graphical content on the web. It does this without using proprietary software. An Internet search for HTML5 will help you to find the latest specification, open-source templates and give you tips on how to use HTML5.

Digital rights management

Digital rights management (DRM) technology allows publishers to embed code in an e-publication that can restrict the use of digital content to those who have purchased the right to use it, or have been authorized by the publisher in some other way. Fears of copyright infringement in the digital marketplace led some publishers to think that DRM was vital to the continued protection of copyright materials, and it continues to be demanded by publishers who are wary of piracy. However, there are now fears that DRM has had unexpected consequences in the battle for market share for e-books. DRM may have a limited life, or will at least require rethinking. Cory Doctorow, an advocate of copyright reform, explains this viewpoint in the quote above.

Discussion questions

1. How is the workflow for digital production different from a purely physical production process?

2. Why are standard such as EPUB3 important?

3. How might DRM be hindering publishers and alienating readers?

4. How can DRM help publishers?

Communication for print and e-publications

The methods used for the physical supply of books from publishers (via distributors, wholesalers, booksellers, libraries and other intermediaries to the end-user) cannot be replicated for digital products. A virtual rather than a physical publication must be sent electronically to the computer, mobile device or e-reader from a server, either by copying a file to the local memory, reading it from its location in the cloud, or streaming it in a way similar to that done with music files. The communication and supply services coalesce, and we might say that this is a manifestation of the 'medium' becoming the 'message'.

Promotion of content or device?

Browsing the Internet is not the same as browsing in a bookshop. Different design elements can be appropriate for the p-version and e-version of the same title – and the online marketing message can contain far more title and author information than could ever have been printed on a physical book jacket or paperback cover. Just as physical covers have always been adapted for different geographic and language markets, e-commerce book displays can use cookies and other profiling devices to target specific market segments, or even individual readers.

When e-books were first produced, the objective of much of the marketing communication was to persuade customers to acquire a proprietary e-reader. In the promotions for Kindle, Nook, iPad and other devices, the marketing message promoted purchase of the devices themselves rather than the content that they might display.

The growth in sales of popular fiction and non-fiction in e-book format is following on from the development of an owner base (much of it the result of gifts). After this initial growth in the number of e-readers in consumers' hands, the message now focuses on the different functionality available from different devices, the range of titles available through the dedicated e-bookstores, and the price. In all of this, brand (Amazon, Kindle, Apple, iPad, Nook) plays an important role.

Publishers in the meantime continued to promote individual authors, titles, genres and series, with the added message that the books were available in the formats that matched the readers' choice of branded device.

Google

Another giant of the digital revolution, Google, has been engaged with publishing-related activities throughout this century. Since its launch in 2004, what is now known as Google Books has scanned and digitized over 15 million books and aims to have over 100 million titles in its databases by 2020. Google's aim is to make out-of-copyright works available free of charge, and to make extracts of copyright protected works available (and more specifically searchable) online under an interpretation of 'fair use'.

6.7
Sales growth
In January 2012, Pew Research reported that sales of tablet computers and e-book readers in the US had surged, causing the share of adults who own either device to nearly double, from 10 per cent to 19 per cent. (Kindle, Kindle Fire and Amazon are trademarks of Amazon.com, Inc. or its affiliates.)

6.7

Google Books has developed through collaboration with major libraries throughout the world, but has been subject to litigation from various bodies representing publishers, authors and other rights holders. The activity of Google Books has also been resisted in the European Union. Google also sell e-books of copyright works through the Google e-book store.

Children's e-books

Some of the first digital books (produced on CD-ROM in the 1990s) were adaptations of children's books. Developing the children's market for e-books with high graphic content (similar in many ways to the games that are already familiar to children) is of benefit to publishers and other content providers, but it has caused debate. Some child psychologists and educationalists including the renowned neuroscientist Susan Greenfield have courted controversy by suggesting that this might be having an effect on children's attention span and the development of cognitive and social skills. (*New Scientist*, 3 August 2011)

Royalties, advances and fees for digital publishing

As we saw in Chapter 4 (see page 102), the contract between the author and the publisher determines the payments to be made for the rights to publish. The development of e-books is bringing about changes in the way that authors are paid. There is a tendency for more authors to be paid on a fee basis, and, when royalties are paid on digital editions, for them to be higher than they are for print books. Authors and their agents also sometimes retain e-book rights and publish in their own right, hoping to take what would have been the publisher's share for themselves.

E-book comics

Comic book apps often appear on the e-book bestseller lists. The combination of striking graphics and short text seem ideal for the medium. Other big sellers are kid's activity books – the *Princess Dress Up* app was a hot title when Prince William married Kate Middleton in 2011.

There are some similarities in both presentation and market between manga, *bandes dessinées*, comic books, graphic novels and the computer games industry, and this kind of e-book is also being adapted for mobile reading.

Special comic viewers have been developed to ensure proper screen display of the graphics. These include Jomic, FFView and Simple Comic.

Comic content lends itself to the integration of text, image, video and interactive games software, and this is developed by both the big media conglomerates and independent graphics houses: they watch each other closely as they manoeuvre to occupy or defend a market share in this growth sector of the digital culture market. Social networking and blogging sites can also be used to generate and manipulate e-book comics.

6.8
Comics
DC Thomson, based in Dundee (Scotland), is the publisher of some of the most popular UK comics, including *The Beano*, *The Dandy* and *Jackie*. Characters from these comics (such as *The Bash Street Kids* pictured here) have appeared in movies, TV programmes and computer games.

6.8

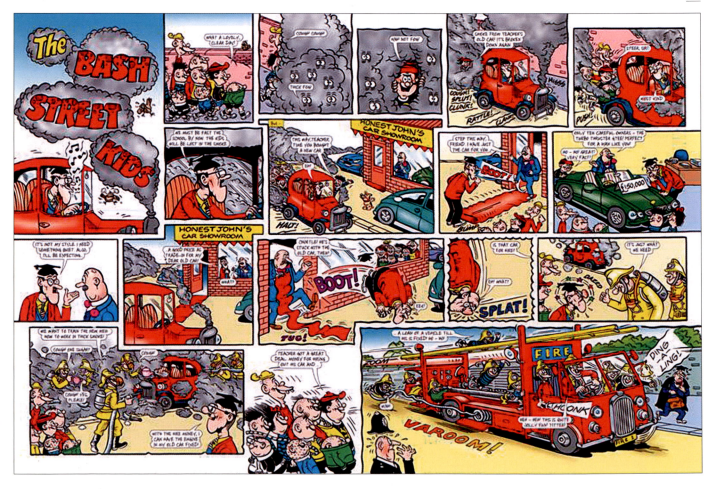

P-book pricing vs. e-book pricing

Some customers have become used to the idea that e-books are cheap, as companies such as Amazon sold them as 'loss leaders' to push the sales of e-readers. Unfortunately, in much the same way as the 'buy one get one free' and 'three-for-two offers' that did such harm to bricks and mortar bookshops, low e-book pricing may affect publishers' financial viability. Pricing of e-books (and the split of revenues between author, e-book distributor and publisher) has been a major issue from the beginning. It soon became clear that readers of e-books were not willing to spend as much on an e-book as they were on a p-book. Some of the early e-book 'bestsellers' were free downloads, and this helped to boost the idea that lots of e-books were being acquired by consumers. Having already bought an e-book reading device, consumers wanted cheaper books, recognizing that publishers were saving on printing, warehousing and fulfilment costs. What they didn't recognize, and what publishers were slow to articulate, is that publishers are not just printers and distributors; they fulfil many other functions that continue to cost money in the digital age: most notably the development of authors and their projects, packaging and brand, marketing and promotion, and long-term customer relationships.

6.9
Espresso Book Machine
The American Book Center in Amsterdam (Holland) uses the Espresso Book Machine to produce POD books for its customers.

6.9

Are customers aware of changes in production technology?

The technology that has changed book production (POD, digital printing, and content processing) has not had an effect on the way most consumers view the printed book. To many book buyers, the quality of POD books is indistinguishable from those produced by letterpress. Short-run digital printing can enable short print runs to be produced for sale through traditional channels, and it is likely to remain as the main production method for illustrated publications in print runs of less than 500.

Inventions like the Espresso Book Machine® (EBM), which makes a paperback book in minutes, have a capacity to produce POD copies on a local basis at point of need, but, in spite of a few machines in large bookshops and at institutions like the World Bank, this technology has not yet become familiar to most consumers.

Discussion questions

1. How have Amazon, Apple and Google had an effect on e-book development?

2. Do bookshops have any future?

3. Is the difference between various e-readers based on technology, networking, consumer communication or brand?

4. How might e-books be particularly suitable for comic books?

Case study: Print and digital at the university presses

University presses may not be the first publishers to come to mind when thinking about publishing innovation, but this sector has long been at the forefront when it comes to developing progressive digital publishing strategies. University presses have three things many commercial publishers do not: extensive and often profitable backlists; a mandate to disseminate research and scholarship not wholly dependent on the profit motive; and human and physical resources of large, stable, technologically advanced institutions. Oxford University Press and Cambridge University Press in the UK, and MIT Press and University of California Press in the US, all have long-established programmes publishing e-journals, books and other materials online.

Oxford University Press

Oxford University Press was a pioneer in some major digital projects in the 1990s, most notably the *Oxford English Dictionary* and the *Oxford Dictionary of National Biography*. Using its digital expertise and ability to finance long-term investment in digital projects, OUP now publishes a wide range of dictionaries and bibliographies online, ELT courses and support materials, and e-versions of major reference materials such as the *Grove Music Online* and *Grove Art Online*.

In 2011 OUP launched University Press Scholarship Online. Starting with more than 7,000 titles in 21 subject areas, from six leading university presses, this service is fully cross-searchable on a single online platform, through the UPSO search engine. But this does not mean that OUP is going a totally digital route. Nigel Portwood, OUP's CEO, commented in 2011 that 'students in the US are going back to school now and they are still buying the print books. We are still not seeing the device penetration in the higher education market that will allow that digital revolution to happen. I know it's coming, but it's a question of whether it's this device or the next one.' ('OUP: new horizons', *The Bookseller*)

Cambridge University Press

Cambridge University Press also has a well-established programme of publishing collections of e-books, and like OUP it launched a new integrated e-book and digital content platform for other academic publishers in October 2011, called University Publishing Online. University Publishing Online will provide libraries with e-books and related database products from a variety of academic publishers worldwide. The service is available to institutions and offers multi-user concurrent access and minimal digital rights management (DRM): customers will be able to buy content once and then own continuing access, or subscribe annually with a subscribe-to-buy facility. Dr Andrew Brown, Director of Academic Publishing at Cambridge University Press, has said: 'A key concept of University Publishing Online is to preserve the individual identity of each of its publishing partners, as every academic press makes a unique contribution to the world of scholarship through its own particular process of selecting, editing and presenting material.' (CUP Press Release, 15 July 2011)

The University of California Press

The University of California Press offers a full range of print and digital publications, working in partnership with numerous external and internal research bodies. It is also a part of the e-scholarship programme at UC, creating a world-class institution-wide resource. For UCP the expertise of the UC library system has proved invaluable in producing an e-publishing platform that covers all sort of texts, including ephemera and grey literature (materials that originate outside of the traditional publishing arena, such as technical reports produced by government agencies), and the library brings with it a culture that understands and values rich metadata. Working with the California Digital Library, it publishes high-quality, certified, UC-sourced scholarship in emerging digital research publication genres. Together, they have launched a collaborative publishing venture, UC Publishing Services, which offers a suite of open access digital and print publication services to University of California centres, institutes, and departments that produce scholarly books. The University of California Press is not only using technology to publish in the digital environment, but also enabling others to do so.

The MIT Press

The MIT Press offers digital books and journals in a variety of formats. They do this themselves through their own e-book store, a journals supply system, electronic collections and searchable online library collections. They also work with some of the leading e-booksellers and content aggregators.

MIT has been a pioneer in making some of its course materials available free online through MIT OpenCourseware (OCW), but this has not been done in collaboration with the MIT Press.

6.10

6.10
University presses online
University press websites reflect their academic nature. These presses have often been at the forefront of digital publishing developments.

Key points

University press publishing can provide some general lessons about how publishing can develop digital publishing alongside the more traditional print formats.

◉ **Investment and scale**: Some university presses are able to undertake large projects that require high levels of investment and a long development cycle because they are less constrained by short-term demands for profit.

◉ **Partnerships and collaborations**: The networks to which these presses belong, both within their own institutions and in the broader academic and scholarly community, enable them to develop long-term collaborations that can focus on joint ambitions for excellence rather than narrow competitive advantage. There is often a wide range of technical expertise available internally, while even larger commercial publishers are frequently reliant on contracting expertise from the external market.

◉ **Searchability and access**: The ethos of universities and academic libraries helps to focus the publisher on issues of searchability and access, driven not by commercial imperatives but more closely tied to the needs of the user rather than his or her potential value as a target for other marketing messages.

◉ **Global reach**: The e-publications of university presses are mostly not subject to territorial market restrictions, so digital distribution to world markets can be easier than in some other areas of publishing. Global reach can also be of importance in developing e-book distribution and aggregation systems that other presses from around the world can take advantage of. In areas such as English-language teaching (ELT), the digital expertise allows university presses to adapt material to specific markets.

Activity

There are numerous university presses, both large and small, in many countries in the world. Conduct an Internet search and look closely at three or four in different countries. For each one, consider the following questions.

1. What evidence is there that the press has a coherent digital strategy?

2. Does the press have collaborations with other departments within the university?

3. Does the press have collaborations with other institutions?

4. Which subject areas appear to be the focus of the e-publishing programme?

5. Why do some subject areas seem particularly suited to the university press e-publishing business model?

Chapter 7

Marketing, sales and distribution

Building on the idea that all publishing should satisfy a need in a target market, this chapter focuses on how all parts of the publishing organization must be aware of the eventual reader or user when they are acquiring, editing, designing and producing a publication. It explores how marketing and the supply chain are interlinked and work together to reach readers, and the ways in which publishers (and authors, agents and other intermediaries) communicate through promotion, publicity and social media. These activities require publishers to be creative in developing, managing and monitoring the budgets and schedules required to put on effective marketing campaigns. This chapter also looks at collecting and analyzing marketing information and using the feedback to market publications successfully.

Marketing

In its broadest sense, marketing is at the core of publishing: it is about the process of telling retailers and readers about the publications that have been developed and ensuring that they are attractive to their target markets. Even the most beautifully written, designed and produced publication has not fulfilled its role if it does not reach its intended audience. So while publications must appeal to an audience and be appropriately priced, delivering them into the hands of readers is vital. This is dependent on two things: communicating effectively with potential buyers and readers (both directly and through a wide variety of intermediaries), and managing the physical or digital supply chain that gets the publication in front of the reader.

7.1

7.1
Reinforcing brand
Print and audio versions of a book are often packaged with the same image and design. This helps the consumer to identify it as the same content, and reinforces brand. Both the book and the audiobook are published by HarperCollins.

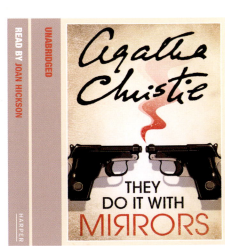

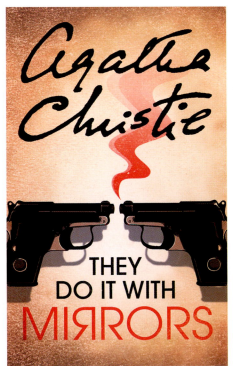

The marketing mix

The traditional four 'Ps' of marketing – product, price, place and promotion – are incorporated in the idea of the marketing mix, a tool that can help publishers to understand the different elements that make it possible to satisfy the consumers' needs, and make enough profit to stay in business.

Product

The product (or service) that is provided must be produced with the qualities and features that the consumer is looking for. Another way of looking at this is in terms of the benefits that the user gets from the product. Does, for example, the book entertain, instruct or otherwise give the reader something that is useful or pleasurable? What does the publication look like? What will the customers think about the format and design? What is the user experience? How the product is made (both physically and digitally) often determines how it is received by the market.

Price

When a price is set for the publication, it must be right for the target market – neither too high nor too low. Customers have an expectation about what they want to pay for a particular product or service and it's important to get it just right: a high price can mean prestige or rip-off, and a low price may indicate cheap and nasty – or a terrific bargain and value for money. Publishers and booksellers are used to selling separate editions (hardback, paperback, and e-book) at different prices, and they are now experimenting with differential pricing for a variety of market segments, and diverse distribution channels.

Pricing is also vital to determining the income that is derived from each sale, and the levels of trade discounts and agency payments must be taken into account. The income must be sufficient to cover all the publisher's costs.

Place

The best place to sell the product must also be considered. How is the physical or digital publication going to be distributed? Do customers have preferences as to where and how they spend their money? Is it necessary to think about different supply channels for distinct market segments? The same book, for example, may sell to different types of reader in a bookshop a supermarket or through an online retailer.

Promotion

The promotion strategy may include e-marketing, social media, print and poster advertising, public relations, sales promotion, events, and reviews. All of this is geared to communicating successfully with identified target markets, other parts of the supply chain and relevant gatekeepers. These gatekeepers are people or organizations that make critical decisions about buying books for the trade, promoting them to their customers, and dealing with other people who influence publicity and promotion in other parts of the chain.

At various times you are certain to see other 'Ps' mentioned as part of the marketing mix – including people, profit and packaging. These are discussed throughout this book.

Supply chain

In recent years the supply chain for both physical and digital publications has developed and changed, and looks set continuing to do so. The main purpose of the supply chain remains that of ensuring a timely and cost-efficient supply from the publisher to the reader. The smooth operation of this supply chain requires not just robust systems to handle the storage and delivery of physical and digital publications, but also a secure system for handling the financial transactions involved in the commerce of book supply.

At all points in the supply chain there are opportunities to develop marketing strengths through publicity, promotion, social networks, communities and more nuanced articulation of brand identities. In this way, the supply chain and the communication chain are intimately and intricately interlinked.

The publisher's warehouse and distribution system

When the printer has completed the production process and the job has been approved by the production controller and the editor, the bulk of the printed stock is sent to the publisher's warehouse, or to the warehouse of the distributor who stocks and distributes the books on the publisher's behalf. The publisher's order processing system has a record of all advance orders placed for the book prior to publication (variously called advance orders, pre-publication orders, subscription orders or 'dues'), and these advance orders are shipped to the retail booksellers, bookstore chains and book wholesalers in time for them to be offered for sale on the official publication date.

Distributors and wholesalers

Distributors warehouse books and act on behalf of the publisher to supply bookshops and wholesalers on terms set by the publisher. They produce sales invoices and collect payment on the publisher's behalf, remitting funds to the publisher on a regular cycle after deducting an agreed service charge, which is usually based on a percentage of the publisher's net sales revenue.

Wholesalers buy books from publishers and sell them on to retail outlets on terms that they agree with these retailers. Many distributors now also offer POD facilities so that publishers' titles are printed out and dispatched by the same companies.

7.2
Amazon distribution
The Amazon warehouse at Milton Keynes, one of a growing number of distribution centres in the UK, has huge capacity and distributes thousands of books each day.

7.2

Both wholesalers and distributors can undertake additional sales and marketing activities for publishers (usually geared specifically to promotion to the trade) and publishers pay for these services. They also provide promotional materials and subsidies for special promotions. Some firms like Gardners Books (UK) and Ingram Book Company (US) offer a variety of these services, from which publishers can choose.

Booksellers find it more cost-effective to use wholesalers as they can then get all their orders from one place in one delivery (often next day). There is just one invoice, and returns of unsold stock can be made to one location with one credit note. Nearly all of the business between publisher, distributor, wholesalers and booksellers is done using web-based communication systems.

Where and how books are sold

Most publishers do not sell printed books directly to their end-users (although an increasing number of publishers now actively pursue sales of e-books directly from their own websites); they deal with booksellers, supermarkets, online retailers, special offers, and clubs by selling to them at a discount or by paying an agency commission.

Publishers, their sales managers and sales representatives have the job of making sure that their company's titles are stocked and displayed prominently in the retail outlets, and that they are part of any in-store promotions organized through the trade. The sales team are in touch with all those who stock and sell physical books: independent bookshops, bookstore chains, supermarkets selling books, and special outlets such as shops at university campuses, tourist locations, museums and art galleries.

Likewise, for online bookselling, publishers make sure that the relevant websites have the necessary information about the publication (see the section on 'metadata' on page 178). They may negotiate appropriate promotion and publicity deals with the Internet retailer, and these deals may entail the publisher granting a higher discount or providing a subsidy payment.

Retail bookselling

The retail book market has undergone radical changes this century, widely seen as resulting from the increase in digital publishing, the growth of sales through non-traditional outlets (supermarkets, online retailers), more direct purchasing by some large retailers, and, in the case of the UK, the end of the system of fixed prices under the Net Book Agreement in the 1990s. Major bookshop chains have ceased trading (Borders) or changed ownership (Waterstones), and many independent booksellers have gone out of business.

In spite of this, publishers still rely on retail booksellers to stock and promote their new titles. Bookshops provide a place where customers can examine the physical books at leisure, and also make unexpected discoveries when browsing the shelves. Buying habits have changed (particularly for the most popular titles), but some independent bookshops are putting up a good fight; and their share of the overall book market is not declining as rapidly as it was.

The most creative bookshops offer something the online retailer cannot, so there has been a big increase in author appearances, book club meetings, local book fairs, readings for children and other special events in bookshops, in order to stress the role of the bookshop in the community as a place where you can meet other people who love reading and know about books.

7.3
Daunt bookshop
Daunt's chain of six bookshops has been a big success in competing with the book chains. So much so, that in 2011 its owner, James Daunt, was appointed managing director of Waterstones by the company's new owner, Alexander Mamut.

7.3

The role of the professional bookseller in knowing the individual taste of customers, recommending or 'hand selling' (as it is known in the US) books, is being emphasized as the great marketing advantage that bricks-and-mortar bookshops still have over sites like Amazon. The challenging market conditions have led to some independent booksellers evolving cooperative ventures between groups of independent booksellers in order to compete with the big chains.

To protect their sales, some booksellers are increasing their stock of remainders (publishers' unsold stocks) and promotional books (specially produced cheap editions), and the market for second-hand and collectible books has grown in recent years. In the UK, charity shops, like the Oxfam Book Shops, have captured a large part of the high-street second-hand market, and this has been identified as another reason for the decline in sales of new books at independent bookshops.

Discoverability and choice

Browsing in a bookshop; reading reviews in the press and online; and recommendations by friends and family have long been important ways that have influenced readers as to which publications to buy, borrow and read. At the same time, a large proportion of books and magazines are bought on impulse. Marketing can be seen as guiding the potential customer through the labyrinth of potential purchases, so understanding how people behave in their role as consumers is very important.

In planning a publicity and promotion campaign, marketers need to understand which recommendations have the voice of authority; how readers' purchasing decisions are influenced by the image they have of themselves and their social group; and how people may change their buying behaviour in different situations (think of the various ways we buy books for work, gifts or when travelling).

Since Chris Anderson publicized the idea of 'the long tail' in *Wired* in 2004, there has been a lot of discussion about the nature of the 'choice' offered by online retailers (like Amazon), book digitization projects (like Google Books) and the proliferation of book bloggers, tweeters and self-publishers. It is now possible to identify and 'find' a much larger amount of published writing than was possible at the beginning of the twenty-first century. However, it is still true that a relatively small number of publications represent a high proportion of the overall sales volume by both units and monetary value. For every million-selling author, there are hundreds of thousands of other writers and journalists with few readers.

Discounts

When they sell to the retail trade, publishers receive less than the price that is printed on the cover of the book or advertised on a website, because the retailers buy the books from the publisher at a discount. This can range from 25–55 per cent on different types of books (less for academic and school books and more for mass-market paperbacks). For books sold to Amazon, Walmart (US) or Tesco (UK), the discount will be up to 70 per cent, meaning the publisher may get no more than 30 per cent of the 'publisher's price'. These high discounts can still leave a profit for the publishers of bestselling consumer books, because of the increase in the numbers of copies sold; but for less popular books and those from publishers with small sales, the greatly increased discounts can make it very difficult to see any profit at all.

In many countries booksellers have the right to send back unsold copies of books to the publisher and receive a full credit; and the issue of 'returns', as they are known, has proved to be another thing that has affected the profitability of publishers. Innovation in alternative marketing is therefore vital for smaller publishers, and those with titles that sell in small quantities.

The economics of trade publishing have changed significantly over the past two decades. When books carried a fixed price, and most sales were through the established book trade or through library suppliers (specialist wholesalers that provide libraries with books), the publisher could expect (after book trade discounts of 20–40 per cent then prevalent) to receive no less than 60 per cent of the list price of the sale from each book sold. The author would usually have got a fixed percentage of the list price of the book (often between 10–15 per cent), or a similar percentage of the publisher's net receipts (the money they actually got from the trade). Even if many books were not as successful as the publisher had hoped, the overall return was usually enough to cover costs and to provide a modest profit. Now that the retailers demand discounts of up to 70 per cent on the list price, and successful authors command high advances, trade books must sell in very high numbers of units to provide the financial return needed for profitability.

Disintermediation

In recent years, changes in the publishing supply and value chain have led to 'disintermediation', in which the creator and consumer are brought closer together by the more direct connections between individuals (with file sharing and other peer-to-peer channels known as P2P); and transactions between publishers and readers can take place without intermediaries (known as business-to-consumer or B2C). This is made possible by the use of digital technologies for content creation, production and distribution.

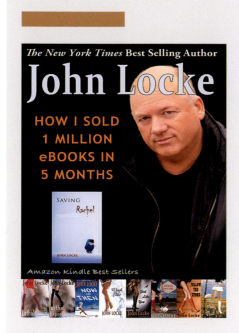

The New York Times Best Selling Author

John Locke

HOW I SOLD 1 MILLION eBOOKS IN 5 MONTHS

SAVING Rachel

Amazon Kindle Best Sellers

The case of John Locke

In 2011 American writer John Locke was the first self-published author to sell a million Kindle e-books. Locke subsequently signed a deal with Simon & Schuster to print and distribute physical copies of his books, while keeping control over his e-book publishing. There are now a number of authors who have achieved million-plus sales of Kindle editions.

Some formerly important links in the book chain have become less important, while other new intermediaries have entered the publishing ecosystem. Publishing networks of writers, readers, and a wide variety of intermediaries act in collaborative and competitive ways that imply we are not so much in a period of 'disintermediation' but one that is 'differently intermediated'. In some cases, authors are brought into closer direct communication with readers through personal appearance and online communications, other intermediaries such as bloggers, special sales promotion agents, and non-traditional book retailers have become more important parts of the book supply network. The term 'diffintermediation' was suggested for this development by Kent Anderson in February 2009 on the website <http://scholarlykitchen.sspnet.org>.

The opportunity for diversity presented by digital publishing is accompanied by a battle to control and influence the Internet as a commercial supply chain, with fierce competition between some major global brands, such as Google, Amazon, Apple, and Facebook. Other media companies, including some of the major newspaper publishers, such as the *Huffington Post* and the *Los Angeles Times*, now produce and distribute e-books. These companies have increasingly sophisticated communication and supply systems, which allow them greater control of the product. Their power can now rival that of the publisher, and much of the marketing activity undertaken by publishers is now centred on working with them, often in ways that have much in common with the business models developed for music streaming, movie rental and multi-player games.

Discussion questions

1. Draw a diagram of the supply chain used to get this book from the publisher to you, the reader.

2. What strategies can smaller publishers use to keep some control over the supply chain?

3. How is the rapid growth in e-book use changing the way books are bought and sold?

4. How can bricks-and-mortar booksellers compete in the current book market?

Communication through promotion and publicity

In order for an audience to discover any publication, there must be effective marketing communication with the potential customers: gatekeepers and networks need to be influenced, and appropriate media must be used for the communications. This brief overview of some of the many types of promotion undertaken by publishers represents a part of the large and varied menu of possibilities.

Publicity and promotion

Promotion and publicity are two types of marketing communication. Publicity is sometimes seen as a 'free' activity, and is generated when other communicators, such as print media, TV, radio reviewers, commentators, and bloggers, are persuaded to tell their audiences about a book, an author or some publishing development. Promotional activities, on the other hand, are those things that have a direct cost, such as space advertising, posters, catalogues, websites, Internet 'features' and banners, TV and radio advertisements.

Both publicity and promotion are important in the communication process, and the distinction between paid and unpaid marketing activities is not always clear. All marketing activity entails cost (direct or indirect), including publicity activities such as book launches, publicity photographs, and author tours. The distinction is blurred further because booksellers and the media often require payment to select a title to be featured as a 'pick' or 'hot tip', and, as a result, the impartiality of reviews on book-related websites and blogs has been questioned. Some reviews are paid for, and others are planted with what is sometimes called 'astroturf' marketing, that is endorsements and positive reviews that are artificially 'planted' when they appear to be authentic 'grassroots' comments. They all form part of marketing.

A marketing toolbox

In planning a marketing campaign for a given publication, some or all of the following might be considered as important ways to communicate with the target audience. Some of these activities are aimed at the audience itself, enticing them to try and buy a particular publication (what is called pull marketing). Some may be geared to increasing the supply and visibility of a publication in the supply chain (called push marketing). By pushing stock and promotional messages through the supply channel, and giving customers reasons to pull the title off the shelves and into their shopping baskets, push and pull work together to create sales.

7.4

7.4
My story so far
UK rap artist
Tinie Tempah's
autobiography is
aimed at a huge fan
base. A whole range
of promotion works
together to create
an irresistible buzz.

Marketing by the product itself

The book as an object (the product itself) carries numerous marketing messages. The cover illustration and design must be chosen with care to reflect both the content and the expectations of the target readers. This includes aspects of design such as the page format, typography, layout, and illustrations.

Dust jacket and paperback covers may contain information on the content, the author, and comparisons to other similar books, favourable comments from other authors, industry experts, or media reviews, and a host of other metadata required for the commercial transaction of book supply (ISBN, barcode, and price). As more book sales are made via the Internet, covers must be attractive and legible as thumbnails, and promotional copy must be readable on screen. The cover may be the most important thing that encourages readers to pick a book off the bookshop shelves or click on a link on a website.

Hyperlinks to sample chapters, author interviews, media tie-ins and author signing schedules that appear on a website promotion must add value to the browsing experience without creating too much distraction from the ultimate objective – to secure a sale.

Promotional materials

Advance information (AI) sheets for new books are produced in both print and digital form for use by sales people, trade intermediaries, and other members of the book network. This AI information represents the basis of the book's metadata.

Catalogues, brochures and flyers (in print, as Internet databases, and as downloads) are produced to promote a wide variety of publications. They are particularly important in specialist markets where direct communication with known customers, or prime prospects, remains a central part of the overall strategy to saturate core markets with communication about publications. This is true of any publishing (such as academic, hobby, or professional) that is aimed at a specific subject group or a limited geographic market. Online catalogues can be used both for reference, and to promote selected new titles, make seasonal offers (such as Christmas, and Mothers' Day) or offer special promotional reduced price sales.

Advertising in the print media promotes awareness of new titles (often in connection with reviews in the same media). Print advertising is a useful way of reinforcing brand awareness for a mass-market title. It can be used to reach specialist markets for niche publications. It also plays a role in recruiting authors from among the readers of these journals and magazines.

Direct mail promotion to potential customers is still a major way in which specialist publishers announce their new publications to the market. Much of this direct promotion and selling is now done via e-mail promotion lists, which reduces costs and can make it easier to gather more valuable information on potential customers.

Video and audio promotions are widely used because of the availability of sites like YouTube, and the possibility of making low-cost podcasts and webcasts. These methods are an extension of the type of publicity that can be gained through personal appearances and readings. The possibility of forwarding links to entertaining or informative videos opens up the possibilities for the viral spread of the promotional message.

7.5
007
When James Bond leapt from the pages of Ian Fleming's novels to the big screen, the success of the cinema adaptation was used to re-promote the books.

7.5

Point-of-sales promotion

In-store promotions include window and point-of-sale (POS) displays in bookshops and other retail outlets. The publisher may subsidize this promotion, often related to an author signing, a reading, or a media launch. The way in which a book is displayed in the bookshop also makes a difference. Promoted books are often exhibited on tables (often as part of special pricing promotions), or face-out, so that the cover design has full effect.

Special promotions are also arranged with Internet and e-book suppliers on a paid basis. Web banners and other online advertising is paid for on the basis of how many people view or click through a particular link or page; these form an important part of the promotional mix.

Physical posters (especially in high traffic areas such as train stations) and display ads in the print media (especially for celebrity and media tie-in books) are still important in reaching some mass audiences, and these can often be downloaded from publisher websites, used as digital wallpaper, or posted on social media. Posters can be particularly important in promoting new titles from established writers, as well as for brand authors who have a regular readership, or books that have TV and movie tie-ins.

Events

Author appearances, live interviews and signings at book festivals, in bookshops and at other events are increasingly important as authors develop as self-promoters and performers. Popular writers must be accessible to their audiences in person as well as online and in the media. While this is not an entirely new phenomenon (Mark Twain and Charles Dickens both undertook punishing author tours across nineteenth-century America), air travel and modern media pressures have made the promotional tour both more gruelling and more effective in reaching a mass audience. These author appearances are important in getting publicity in local media for new titles by established and upcoming authors, and help to establish the all-important 'platform' that is a foundation of any author's brand identity.

Exhibitions at conferences, trade shows and professional events provide important promotional and publicity opportunities to professional, academic and STM publishers. Hobby publishers also have exhibitions and sales counters at specialist events like food fairs, motor rallies, and boat shows. These events represent an effective way of joining a specialist community, and this is good not only for sales, but also to keep ahead of trends and to recruit new authors.

7.6

Book fairs such as BookExpo in the US and the Guadalajara International Book Fair in Mexico are used for selling books to booksellers and rights to other publishers, and to link with companies providing other services, such as IT systems, shipping and logistics, and printing.

Other book events, such as literary festivals, are intended for the general public and to generate publicity for authors. The Hay Festival, which started in Hay-on-Wye in the UK, is now a global organization hosting literary events in place such as Kerala in India and Xalapa in Mexico.

7.6
Kolkata Book Fair
Publishing companies at book fairs promote their books to the general public and to the book trade.

7.7

The LongPen
Margaret Atwood has championed the 'LongPen' by which authors can do book signings using an automated pen connecting author and reader via the Internet.

Media publicity

Reviews and author features in the press remain a major form of book publicity. In some cases, the book pages of daily and weekly newspapers have been downgraded (with shorter reviews of a less varied selection of books) and supplemented by blogs, podcasts and social media feeds.

Serialization, readings and adaptations of books in newspapers, magazines and on the radio are another valuable means of promoting books (mostly fiction and popular non-fiction). This is not just an integral part of the marketing mix, but also a source of additional revenue for the publisher and the author.

Sample chapters and free e-books have joined the promotional toolkit, and free e-books are sometimes offered in the press and through book websites. Chapters of forthcoming books are also made available online and at the back of paperback editions of popular fiction.

Communities, viral marketing and 'free' publicity

Web promotion can be used to generate an e-mail list, to develop a social network community, or to support promotional activities such as personal appearances and media events. Publishers' websites and social media are in stiff competition for the attention of the browser, so the purpose of a publisher's Internet activity must be well planned (but flexible). It should be aimed at achieving specific goals, and be checked to see if these goals are achieved.

Publishers' digital promotion activities include techniques that go beyond the features available in print brochures, posters and point-of-sale handouts. Digital marketing can engage potential customers by getting them to 'play' on the site (referred to as 'gamification') and by encouraging them to enter competitions, answer quizzes, watch promotional videos or download sample chapters, share content via email or social networking sites, and add comments or reviews.

Customers may be persuaded to register for email alerts, which can give the publisher information about the users if they complete a profile. An item that is tweeted, forwarded or otherwise recommended to others can spread like a virus (which is why it's called viral marketing).

Whatever the online marketing strategy, it is vitally important to monitor usage and analyze data on a regular basis. By using tools such as Google Analytics you can see if you are reaching your target audience effectively and also discover if any groups you had not previously considered are finding your site interesting. Remember that the number of visitors to a site or page is not nearly as important as who they are, how often they visit, how long they stay and what they do while on your site.

Authors also actively promote themselves and their works on the Internet. They may encourage other sites to review, promote and provide what appears to be disinterested word-of-mouth recommendations to appropriate market segments. Many other parts of the book chain (agent, publisher and media) may contribute to the digital marketing campaign. This is important in specialist markets where the academic, professional, hobby or enthusiast websites and social media may be the most effective way of reaching the audience. In the mass market, instant trending can result from a skilful spread of a Twitter hashtag or viral video.

Marketing brands

Brand is increasingly important to publishers. Elsevier, Mills and Boon, Harlequin, Scholastic, Norton, and Virago are all examples of successful publisher branding. Each represents a certain style of publishing, a mark of quality, a reason for the book buyer to trust that a publication bearing one of these imprints will deliver according to expectations. Trusted brands reduce the feeling of risk inherent in every purchase.

A publisher's trademark is only one of the important brand elements: authors and characters are also important, for example, the author Lee Child and his character Jack Reacher (published by Random House), Ian Fleming and his hero James Bond. Imprints and series are also brands, for example, *Teach Yourself* books and *Horrible Histories*. In these cases, publishers consciously develop the brand identity and use it to communicate with loyal readers and to develop new audiences. '*Buy this book about this character written by this author in this series published by this publisher and you won't be disappointed,*' the marketing message might run.

Brands are about building trust, loyalty and repeat purchase. They encourage word-of-mouth promotion, which is so important to sales growth, and encourage a sense of community that comes from brand loyalty.

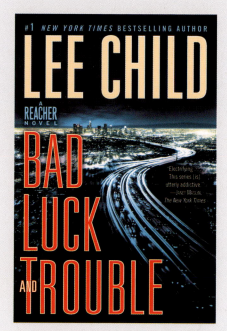

#1 NEW YORK TIMES BESTSELLING AUTHOR
LEE CHILD
A REACHER NOVEL
BAD LUCK AND TROUBLE

'Electrifying. This series (is) utterly addictive.'
—JANET MASLIN, *The New York Times*

As parts of the supply network focus on blockbusting bestsellers, and employ marketing techniques to maximize revenue, 'brand' authors are expected to play their part, often undertaking gruelling schedules of interviews, personal appearances and media performances. Those authors from whom lower sales are anticipated are largely expected to do a lot of promotion themselves, manage their own websites, and arrange local readings and signing sessions.

Digital product placement

The idea of digital product placement was promoted so that different products could 'appear' on-screen in TV programmes, depending on the audience or market. So, for example, brands of breakfast cereal on sale in different countries can be substituted on the breakfast table in a TV drama. This technique is now being suggested for e-books. So a product might be inserted into the digital text according to the location where the book is being read, the preferences of the reader or a promotion in an online or neighbouring store – all will provide payments for the publisher and author. At a flick of the digital publisher's switch, James Bond's car could change from an Aston Martin to a Ferrari to a Bentley, and Paddington Bear could eat peanut butter instead of marmalade.

Metadata and cataloguing

Metadata is the information that enables a published item to be identified, located and accessed from among the mass of other published items available in an ever more varied choice of formats. It's often described as 'data about data'. An extension of the kind of information that might be found in a library catalogue for a given publication, metadata includes a wealth of other information for which a common terminology and format is essential if there is to be effective communication between the different data systems that connect parts of the publishing network.

The management of metadata is now seen as a central function of publishing. It includes the more obvious details such as the author, title, publisher, place of publication, information on print and digital formats, unique identifiers such as the ISBN, ISSN, and DOI, and can include the markers needed for DRM.

Good metadata is an aid to effective online searching for traditional catalogue information such as the title, author, ISBN, price, publication date, and blurb, and for tags and keywords that promote discoverability and improve the success of the SEO (Search Engine Optimization) strategy. Many parts of the publishing organization are now involved in making sure that the 'data about data' is accurate and organized in a way that helps readers to discover the publication through whatever search and retrieval method they employ.

Industry information

Nielsen BookData, which calls itself 'the primary bibliographic provider for book product metadata services to book trade customers in the UK and around the world', stresses that digital books need product metadata as much as physical books do to fulfil the objectives below.

◉ Enable the discovery of each separately traded product.

◉ Persuade and inform the customer showing clearly details of characteristics of the work identified.

◉ Enable unambiguous selection and sale of the chosen product.

◉ Enable the supply chain to understand what has been sold and when.

For more information, you can consult the websites of Nielsen BookData and the Book Industry Study Group, which produces a comprehensive 'Roadmap of Organizational Relationships' and a 'Roadmap of Identifiers'.

Some types of metadata

◉ The DOI – Digital Object Identifier – is used to identify a component such as text, an image, or other media.

◉ The ISBN – International Standard Book Number – identifies a particular manifestation or edition of a book.

◉ ISSN – International Standard Serial Number – identifies a journal.

◉ Metadata also includes ways of identifying a particular part of the distribution channel such as the SAN – Standard Address Number.

An expert's view of serendipity

'Serendipity is the great unsung hero of publishing. We can never be sure of the precise value of all those sales arising from chance encounters in bookshops, the flash of a good jacket catching the reader's eye, igniting the purchase instinct so that before they know it they've bought another book. We've all been there; we've casually browsed, and probably found many of our favourite books this way – by chance, in bookshops, passing time, scanning idly. We will never have a precise figure for what this is worth, but it is likely to be very large indeed.

How about in digital environments? Well, there has been a great attempt at not just replicating the mechanisms of the physical world but surpassing them, and a good deal of web innovation has centred around recommendation engines, affiliate networks, filtering systems, automatic suggestions and the prediction of taste, a world where our literary preferences are served up to us, where we always find what we want. To some this is a world where abundant culture becomes easily discoverable, where we can find what we like and structure our experience in a totally customized way; to others it is what Eli Pariser has called the "filter bubble", an egotistical echo chamber where we are never challenged by newness or difference aside from our pre-existing predilections.

Regardless of the rights or the wrongs, one thing is clear: that in an environment where chance is lost, where algorithms replace luck and the keyword search term is king, metadata is the fulcrum of discovery. Metadata, in short, decides whether your book is found, and by extension whether your book is bought.

Metadata influences search, it influences territoriality and categorization – metadata is the advert, the sales pitch, the sell and the advance promotion; metadata is the random book left on the table, the fervent recommendation of a friend, the arresting blurb, the good review, serving the random browser and the determined buyer alike.

Bad metadata means your book is invisible and un-purchasable. Yet compared with too many industries either totally or increasingly focused on digital commerce, publishing lags in its understanding of SEO practices, metadata standards implementation, data collection and analysis and systems investment.

Yes, most publishers have started all the above. But this is only the beginning. We still haven't fully figured out how to replace the experience of shopping in a bricks-and-mortar store, that sense of surprise, fun, the unexpected – and we haven't worked out how we can create and capture those impulse buys. We are going to need to, and the answer will be found in a revolution of what metadata we supply, and how we supply it.'

Michael Bhaskar, Digital Publishing Director, Profile Books; on Frankfurt Book Fair Blog

Discussion questions

1. What promotion and publicity techniques would be most suitable for a celebrity cookery book?

2. Why do publishers go to conferences and exhibitions?

3. What is metadata and why is it important?

4. Why is 'discoverability' important?

Managing budgets and schedules

Sales projections for new titles start with the editor's initial evaluation of the market potential and are developed in consultation with sales, marketing and finance departments. They gradually become more detailed as publication day approaches. The sales expectations (in units, monetary value, and in terms of the period over which they are made) both determine and are determined by the promotional plan and the budget that is available. The schedule and budget relate to the potential for sales and profit, and other factors such as the project's overall importance to the company, support from media and parts of the supply chain, and the possibility of significant income from subsidiary rights and export sales.

General and specific costs

Developing and managing a sales and marketing budget and schedule is a vital part of the marketing department's activities; and this is done in the light of the company's expectation of the percentage of its sales revenue that is allocated to this activity. This can range from five to 15 per cent of overall sales revenues depending on the type of publishing and the competitive nature of the particular market.

Some marketing expenses, such as the catalogue, the company's website, and attendance at major book fairs (for example, London, Frankfurt, and Beijing), are undertaken at some level by most publishers. In the planning process, these activities and their costs are often hotly debated; and, as they are central to the company's business, they are planned with great attention to detail.

Other costs, associated with the promotion of particular titles or series, can be broken down and the costs allocated directly to those titles and/or series that are covered. The priorities given to publications in terms of anticipated sales and financial returns, as well as competitive pressures, decide the promotional expenditure.

Marketing budget

The marketing and promotion budget is allocated (see the chart opposite which is an example of an imaginary publishing company's marketing budget) in relation to the company's projected sales revenue (**A**). A proportion of the total marketing budget (**B**) is allocated to central promotion costs (**C**), promoting all the company's new and backlist lists. Each division also has a marketing budget (**D**), which is allocated to the marketing of individual titles, series and lists depending on the publishing programme. Some titles (stars) get a larger proportion of the overall spend (**E**), while other new titles have much less money spent on individual promotion (**F**).

	Breakdown of expenditure	Revenue projected £/$/€	Marketing budget £/$/€
Company	**Company budget** Marketing budget is 5% of the total sales revenue.	**Company revenue (A)** 10,000,000	**Company marketing budget (B)** 500,000 (5% of projected revenue)
	Central promotion costs Includes catalogues, trade fairs, website and backlist promotion.	10,000,000 is the total of the company's projected revenue from the sale of new and backlist titles.	**Company-wide marketing (C)** 250,000 (2.5% of projected revenue)
Division	**Division (5 divisions in company)** Includes exhibitions in major areas of publishing (e.g. STM, art), brochures, ads, and inserts in specialist media.	**Divisional revenue plan** 2,000,000 (x5)	**Divisional marketing budget (D)** 50,000 per division (x5)
Title	**Star titles (3 titles per division)** Includes launch party, author tour, ads, and posters.	**Revenue projections** Each 'star' title: 200,000 Division: 600,000 Company: 3,000,000	**'Star' title marketing budget (E)** Each 'star' title: 10,000 Division: 30,000 Company: 150,000
	Other titles (20 new titles per division) Includes flyers, readings at bookstores, exhibits at specialist events.	**Revenue projections** Each other title: 50,000 Division: 1,000,000 Company: 5,000,000	**Other title marketing budget (F)** Each other title: 1,000 Division: 20,000 Company: 100,000

Marketing schedule

Promotional and publicity activities are carefully scheduled, generally in relation to the publication date, a critical sales period (such as Christmas or the beginning of term or semester), or another significant event.

The detailed schedule is planned at the later stages of the development of the publishing project and, as all promotion and publicity events take time to organize, this planning stage is very important. When the title goes into production, the plan is further refined and expenditure is approved. The expected costs of all activities must be based on real estimates, and from suppliers, such as designers and printers of promotional materials, travel and costs for author events and exhibitions.

Sales staff may have special requirements for promotional materials (such as price lists and display cards), and these are discussed at sales conferences. Overseas agents may want promotional materials, and the international sales team needs time to contact agents and booksellers worldwide. Rights managers also require material to send to other publishers.

Attention to detail is vital, and any metadata (such as ISBNs) and pricing information must be checked carefully. All of this takes time, so a structured schedule is important to ensure that the process goes smoothly and that materials for new titles are prepared well before the publication date.

Discussion questions

1. Who within the company may have a need for promotional materials?

2. What different activities are covered by the promotional budget?

3. When is a promotional schedule prepared?

4. Will a publisher spend an equal amount on promotion of all titles?

Using feedback to monitor success

Now frequently known as metrics, the data sources that publishers need to monitor their business performance have vastly improved over the past two decades. As the supply chain becomes integrated using web-based systems, this information is likely to become even more comprehensive and analytical.

Nielsen BookScan

Nielsen BookData was mentioned earlier in this chapter; another part of the same corporation called Nielsen BookScan collects retail sales information directly from point-of-sale systems in more than 31,500 bookshops around the world. Subscribers can access the data online, and produce a wide variety of reports on such things as market size and share of different book categories, unit sales and revenue for individual publishers, specific imprints, authors and price points. The system gathers information from the supply chain and covers different parts of the market including specialized categories and small imprints, as well as larger companies. BookScan's main focus is on the UK, USA, Australia and New Zealand, but data is available from some other countries.

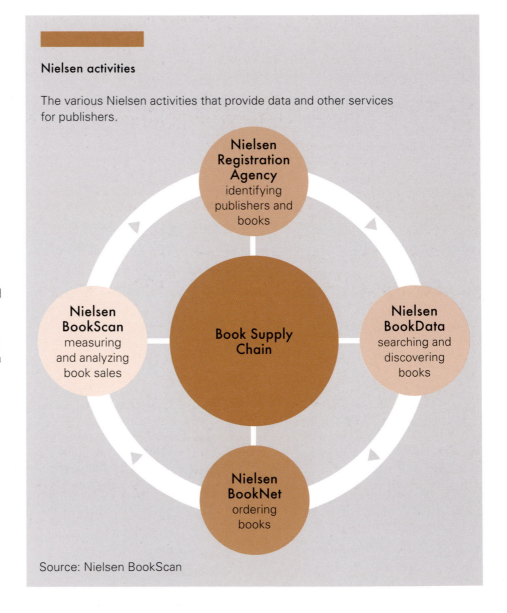

Nielsen activities

The various Nielsen activities that provide data and other services for publishers.

Source: Nielsen BookScan

Keeping an eye on major book buyers

Market research into publishing and bookselling has shown that a quite small core of heavy book buyers (those buying more than 12 books per year) is critical to the health of the business. In 2011 it became clear that these buyers were also among the heaviest buyers of e-books, and that e-books were particularly attractive to the over-50s.

The baby-boomer generation were a major factor in the growth of the trade paperback, the chain bookstore and the growth of reading groups; they may also be at the forefront of the move from p-books to e-books (*The Bookseller*, 8 April 2010). This insight into the way in which a major customer group has changed its buying habits is a good example of the need for publishers and booksellers to watch the way people discover, buy, read and evaluate books.

The book market is rarely static and is prone to periods of rapid development when disrupted by economic, social, political or technological changes. The global economy has an effect on publishing as it does on everything else; and technological developments continue to revolutionize all communications, bringing great changes to the currently evolving hybrid print/digital culture.

Bestseller lists

Publishers of trade fiction, children's books and non-fiction titles benefit when their books appear in bestseller lists. The very word 'bestseller' is often used in advertising and promotion materials, and publishers use the buzz created by the 'bestseller' tag to promote authors and books through the press and other media. This ensures the continued prominent display of the 'bestselling' book in bookshops and online bookselling sites.

Bestseller lists appear in the press, but there is no standard way of determining this status. In some countries, the bestseller lists are based on sales records taken from quite a small sample of publishers or booksellers.

Nielsen BookScan bestseller lists, based on a wide sample of books sold in a given period, can be far more reliable than a more restricted sampling of bookstores and online retailers. Bookstore displays often include what are referred to as 'bestsellers', although the evidence for the bestseller status is sometimes obscure. The rise of e-books has further complicated the way in which bestseller charts are created, but the media now publish lists of e-book bestsellers and some have integrated e-books into the overall bestseller lists.

Discussion questions

1. How does Nielsen BookScan collect data? Why might publishers be willing to pay for the market information that Nielsen gathers?

2. Why is the 'bestseller' label important?

3. Are older people interested in e-books? Why might this group be particularly important to publishers, and how could they tailor their products to meet the needs of the 'baby-boomer' generation?

4. Do e-books appear on bestseller lists?

Case study:

Persephone

Books

Persephone Books – a small publisher with traditional publishing values – shows the importance of keeping control over the communication and supply channels.

Persephone, founded by Nicola Beauman in 1999, publishes novels, short stories, diaries and cookery books. It has developed a reputation for high-quality publishing (in both the content and form), while developing innovative design and marketing. The books are much praised for their clear typographic design, stylishly understated dove-grey jackets, fabric-patterned endpapers and bookmarks, and their entertaining and informative introductions. It has approximately 100 titles currently in print.

The company says its titles are 'chosen to appeal to busy women who rarely have time to spend in ever-larger bookshops and who would like to have access to a list of books designed to be neither too literary nor too commercial', and the company is thriving in its niche market.

7.8

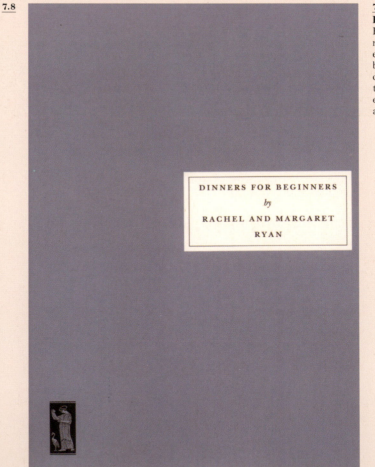

7.8
Persephone cover
Persephone is admired not just for its editorial integrity, but also for its stylish covers, tasteful typesetting, individual endpapers, bookmarks, and quality paper.

The feminist publishing context

Persephone occupies a position within a tradition of women's publishing that came to prominence in the late twentieth century. In the 1970s a number of women's presses were established, reflecting developments in the feminist movement and an increase in academic and media interest in writings by and for women. In the UK, the most famous of these is Virago, founded as an independent publisher in 1973 and now an imprint of Little, Brown Book Group.

Virago publish some of the major feminist thinkers including Kate Millett, Adrienne Rich, Eva Figes, Angela Carter, Juliet Mitchell, Lynne Segal, Sheila Rowbotham, and Elaine Showalter. The Virago Modern Classics list is dedicated to the rediscovery and reprinting of the works of women writers. It has published such diverse authors as George Eliot, Grace Paley, Elizabeth von Arnim, Pat Barker, Edith Wharton, Mae West, Willa Cather and Molly Keane. It has some 200 titles in print.

Virago Travellers is another highly successful series, it has reprinted the stories of the greatest women travellers including Gertrude Bell, Emily Eden, Lucie Duff Gordon, and Lady Mary Wortley Montagu.

In recent years, Virago Vs was launched to cater for a new generation (broadly aimed at 20–35 year olds). The first title was Sarah Waters's tale of Victorian lesbian London, *Tipping the Velvet*.

Other publishers, such as The Women's Press in the UK and the independent US non-profit The Feminist Press, began by rescuing lost and forgotten works by women writers from diverse ethnic, racial and class backgrounds. Some feminist publishers have also been active in publishing books classified as lesbian, gay, bisexual, and transgender (LGBT).

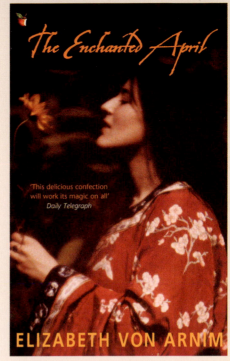

7.9　　　　　　　　　　**7.9**
Virago
For many years, Virago books used distinctive covers with a green band that were instantly recognized by their core readers, but the company now uses a wider variety of designs and images as the books compete in a broader market.

'There are cute books, there are beautiful books and then there are Persephone books.'

The Irish Times

Key points

Women buy more books than men (*2009 US Book Consumer Demographic and Buying Behaviours Annual Report*, Bowker), and the sales of books written by and for women has grown into a significant part of the overall publishing market. Smaller companies publishing for these readers have had to adopt innovative approaches in order to secure sales.

◉ Perspehone is in a market niche where one publisher, Virago, has a commanding visibility and brand strength. In order to compete, Persephone has developed a strong distinctive image of its own, and has successfully used design and direct communication with customers to stress its distinctive identity.

◉ Marketing, sales and distribution remain firmly under Persephone's direct control.

◉ The mail-order strategy is central to Persephone's sales. A regular printed catalogue is distributed, there is a fortnightly newsletter and the company has subscribers who sign up to receive a new book every month for six or 12 months. The website acts as the hub for the Persephone audience and is geared to developing a real community of readers.

◉ Some booksellers do not consider that the tastefully understated Persephone cover designs are suitable for display and promotion through the trade, so the company has issued a small selection of Persephone Classics in illustrated covers for distribution through bookshops. This has been done carefully, making sure not to offend the core market's passion for the classic Persephone design.

◉ Audiobooks (as both CD and MP3 download) are available through the Persephone website, and ten titles were published as e-books for the 2011 Christmas season. As with all its innovations, this is being implemented gradually and with constant review and evaluation.

◉ The Persephone shop is in the same building as the company's office, and harks back to the days when all London publishers had a trade counter, to make sure books were available to customers at all times, even though (due to book trade conventions at the time) publishers did not then sell directly to the public.

◉ All of this shows how important it is for a publisher to keep a constant eye on quality, stay in close touch with readers, and retain control of the supply chain. As Nicola Beauman says: 'The most important thing for us is resuscitating forgotten women writers and having a mail order niche has been a good way to do this.'

Activity

Small publishers often have to be more creative about their marketing than their larger competitors. They must find a memorable way to communicate in the crowded marketplace, make the most of limited budgets and develop a brand in their niche market.

Search online, on bookstore shelves or through your own book collection to identify some small publishers. Find out about their current marketing activities and consider the following questions.

1. What niche market does the publisher target with its promotion?

2. Does the publisher have a brand identity and how is this presented to potential readers and customers?

3. Does the company employ any innovative or special promotional techniques?

4. What is the company's online marketing strategy?

5. How does the company make use of other media in its promotional activities?

Conclusion

The second decade of the twenty-first century is an exciting time to develop a career in publishing. In this book, we have explored how publishing is adapting to the digital culture and the frenetic pace of change that has recently engulfed the industry.

When choosing a career in publishing, it is important to develop professional skills and industry knowledge, and to retain a strong desire to learn about what is happening in the world of books. It is also vital to keep abreast of the industries with which publishing works, and to be aware of the technological developments that may have an impact in the near and mid-term. Developing your career will mean continuing to explore, to analyze and to learn.

Important though technology is, people are at the core of publishing. Without the creative talents of authors, illustrators and designers, there will be no new, thought-provoking and innovative ideas expressed through words and images – the content of successful publishing.

The agents and editors who provide the vision, support, sensitivity and attention to detail necessary to transform the creative content for the reader need a professionalism that is founded on a deep and sensitive knowledge of human nature. The same goes for all aspects of the publisher's communication with readers, booksellers, reviewers, and all the many parts of the network that needs to function efficiently for publishing to be successful.

At the technical level of information processing, production and the logistics of storage and supply, personal relationships, clear and unambiguous communication, and a trustworthy business ethic are required. Production methods in publishing (as in any industry that converts raw materials into saleable goods) can have very negative environmental effects. Some publishers are now much more aware of their responsibility and are applying sustainability criteria when purchasing paper, printing, transportation and server farm facilities.

High ethical standards are unlikely to be sustained in any enterprise without leadership from senior management, who take responsibility for a transparent and equitable financial regime. The roles and responsibilities of people in publishing will adapt and change, but they will still be doing what humans can do best – exploring, adapting, interacting, cooperating and taking joint responsibility for their actions.

The importance of publishing, whatever the medium or technology employed, remains rooted in the importance of communication in our personal, social, cultural and economic lives. The digital culture has given more people the opportunity to express themselves in public, to use social media and to contribute to an explosion of visual and textual material available on the Internet. Where publishers make a difference is in the choices that they make about what to publish and promote, how they engender debate and analysis of important issues, and suggest structures in the way that knowledge and understanding are presented. With so many more words and images available to the reader and viewer, this publishing role becomes even more vital.

'How books will be produced and delivered, who will do what and how they will do it, what roles the traditional publishers will play (if any) and where books will fit in the new symbolic and information environments that will emerge in years to come – these are questions to which there are, at present, no clear answers.'

John B. Thompson, Merchants of Culture, *Polity, 2010*

However, if publishers are to undertake this role in the future, they must retain and constantly reinforce their commitment to another of the pillars of good publishing. They must check facts rigorously to ensure the accuracy of any information presented; monitor the use of language and design elements for clarity of expression and meaning; and focus on delivering a publication to readers that satisfies (and even raises) their expectations.

Publishers are a vital part of society. They are often among the first to speak out for human rights and social justice, to insist that information is not suppressed and that a wide variety of opinion is heard. This responsibility is one that remains important in a world affected by political and social upheaval, climate change and ecological crisis. It is vital that publishers continue and enhance this role, while balancing the tension that sometimes exists between protecting human rights and preserving the right to freedom of expression.

No one knows what publishing will be like by 2050, but it will still be there in some form. What it looks like and how it contributes to the human experience will largely depend on the people who are now just starting their careers in publishing.

Glossary

AA: author's alterations
When an author checks proofs they may make alterations to the text. Publishers do not expect authors to make many changes at this stage in the production process, and if the author insists on making significant changes, the contract may lead to some of the cost of changes being charged to the author.

Advertorial
Published material that is paid for such as advertising, but which may appear to be unbiased editorial content.

Agency model
Under the agency model, e-book prices are set by publishers, with the e-booksellers acting as agents for the publishers. The e-bookseller typically takes 30 per cent commission on the sales price and passes the remaining 70 per cent to the publisher. Author royalties for e-book sales under the agency model are typically 25 per cent of the publisher's NSR.

Application
Personal computers, tablets and other mobile devices use application software that enables them to be used as e-readers. The application (which may be proprietorial or open source) means that e-books can be downloaded and read. Applications such as Apple's iBookstore also act as 'bookstores' that sell access to e-books.

Back list
The part of a publisher's list (as opposed to the new or front-list titles) that is composed of previously published books, some of which may still be good sellers.

BD (bandes dessinées)
A type of comic strip book originating in France and Belgium. The major annual event of BD is the Festival International de la Bande Dessinée d'Angoulême.

Book chain
A way of envisioning a business model in which several distinct groups (such as writers, publishers, printers, booksellers, libraries, and readers) work together as consecutive links of a chain to ensure that books get from author to editor to designer to production to sales, marketing and distribution.

Bouquiniste
Dating from the sixteenth century, the *bouquinistes* of Paris are booksellers of used and antiquarian books who have stalls along the banks of the River Seine.

Bulk
The bulk of a paper stock is a relative measure of the thickness as related to the basic weight of a sheet. Lower bulk reduces opacity. Higher bulk increases the overall thickness of a book.

Bundle
A collection of digital, or print and digital, content that is sold outright or as a subscription at a total price for the package.

Calliper
The thickness of paper when measured with a micrometer. Calliper (US: caliper) is measured in micrometres (1/1000 of a mm), or in the US also in mils (1/1000 of an inch).

CC: Creative Commons
This organization provides tools for creators of intellectual property to keep their copyright while allowing certain uses of their work. CC licences help creators to retain copyright while allowing others to copy, distribute, and make some uses of their work – at least non-commercially.

CIF: carriage, insurance and freight
If sales are made CIF, then the purchaser pays for all shipping costs from the moment the shipment leaves the shipping point, which may be the printer or distributor's warehouse.

CIP: cataloguing in publication
In most countries the national library, such as the British Library, Library of Congress or Bibliothèque Nationale, has the responsibility for cataloguing every new publication in that country, and publishers are required to submit information on new publications to the national library. This cataloguing information, known as cataloguing in publication, is issued prior to publication so that it can be included on the copyright page in the publication.

Cloud
Cloud computing refers to the storage of data and software in the Internet 'cloud' in server farms, rather than on the user's own computer or on a specified, known or static server. Google, Amazon and other publishing-related companies have developed the idea of cloud computing to enable customers to keep their personal libraries of e-books in the 'cloud'. They can then access every title from various devices at any time without the need to transfer data between them.

CMYK: cyan, magenta, yellow, black
These are the four process colours that are used to reproduce colour illustrations in colour printing. These colours are called subtractive colours and can be combined to make the primary colours, red, green and blue (also referred to as RGB). Black is referred to by the letter K as black is the 'key' to which the other colours are aligned (and it avoids confusion with blue).

CTP: computer to plate
A process whereby images (text and illustrations) are placed directly on the printing plate with no need for the intermediary process of making a photographic film. This process reduces costs and produces a sharper image.

Digital native
Someone who was born after the general spread of digital communications and information technology (such as personal computers and mobile phones) into everyday life. Digital natives have used such technology throughout their lives, and so find less difficulty in adapting to further rapid technological changes.

DOI®: digital object identifier
The DOI system is a way of identifying specific units of content and DOI names are assigned to any entity for use on digital networks. This name will not change even if the object to which it refers is moved to, say, another server or owner.

DPI: dots per inch
A measure used to indicate the resolution of a printed image, the quality for the reproduced image being higher the more dots per inch. The term DPI is still used by many printers, although the actual measurement in digital printing is usually in pixels per inch (PPI).

DRM: digital rights management
Any technology that publishers use to restrict the use of digital content to those who have purchased the right to use the content or have been authorized by the publisher in some other way. DRM is considered by some to be central to the continued protection of copyright materials and other IP in the digital world.

DTP: desktop publishing
The term desktop publishing was introduced in the late twentieth century when typesetting and design software such as QuarkXPress and InDesign became commonly used by publishers. Most publications are now produced using such software.

E-book
An increasingly popular format for publications in which they are produced as digital files that can be downloaded from the Internet or stored in the 'cloud' and be read on a variety of e-readers, tablets, mobile devices or personal computers.

EFL: English as a foreign language
EFL publishing is a major business for UK publishers, who sell and license EFL programmes in many countries of the world.

ELT: English language teaching
ELT is a term generally used interchangeably with EFL.

EPS: encapsulated PostScript
An electronic file format (an extension of Adobe® PostScript® 3™) used for storing graphics and for transmission of graphics files to the printer. EPS files can be made from TIFF or JPEG files and the advantage of EPS graphics is that they can be scaled to any size without loss of detail.

EPUB
EPUB3, released in September 2011, is the latest version of EPUB, the most common standard used when formatting e-books. EPUB3 increases the support for a wider range of publication requirements, including complex layouts, rich media, interactivity, and global typographic features. EPUB3 is utilized for a broad range of digital content, including books, magazines and educational, professional and scientific publications.

E-publishing
Digital publication is also known as e-publishing, particularly when used in reference to books and magazines published for distribution through commercial channels such as Kindle, Apple iBooks and Kobo.

E-reader
The devices used to read e-books and other digital publications. Some of these are dedicated e-readers such as the Kindle and the Nook, while other devices such as the iPad and personal computers can also be used as e-readers.

E-reading
Reading text (and images) on a computer, tablet, e-reader or other portable reading device.

Extent
The number of pages contained in a publication.

Fair use
The principle that a certain limited amount of copyright material can be reproduced in another publication without the need to obtain the copyright holder's permission. Principles of fair use differ from country to country.

F&G: folded and gathered
During the production process, most books are printed on sheets containing 16 or 32 pages. These sheets are then folded and gathered into F&G signatures or sections which will then be sewn or glued together to form the complete book block.

FOB: free on board
When a shipment is made FOB, the shipper pays for all shipping costs up to the point when it is loaded onto the ship or aeroplane, and more generally (particularly in the US) determines any point where responsibility for the goods is transferred from the seller to the buyer.

FSC: Forest Stewardship Council
The FSC certifies paper that has been sourced from well managed and sustainable forests. Many publishers now have a policy of using FSC certified paper whenever possible.

Graphic novel
Fictional stories published in comic-strip format. This is a popular format, with bestsellers like Art Spiegelman's *Maus: A Survivor's Tale*.

Grid
Designers use a grid in both physical and computer design to organize text and images.

GSM: grams per square metre
GSM (sometimes gm^2) is used as a measure of the weight (or substance) of paper. Most books are printed on papers between 75 and 115 gsm.

Halftone
A reprographic technique that uses dots of various sizes to reproduce images. The term is also used for images produced by this process.

House style
Publishers usually establish a house style for language use (such as spelling and punctuation) in order to ensure consistency, and for design (such as formats, page layouts) to support marketing and reinforce brand identity.

HTML: hypertext markup language
HTML is the most common mark-up language used for web pages. It is written using tags like <style>, <head> or <title> (always in angle brackets), within the web page content. You can look at the source code of most web pages by clicking on 'view source code'.

HTML5
A development of the HTML markup language that has numerous new features designed to make it easy to include and handle multimedia and graphical content on the web.

Imposition
The arrangement of individual pages on the printing plate used to print the sheet, that is then folded and gathered to form a section or signature of a publication. The pages must be 'imposed' so that they appear in the correct order when the sheet is folded. There are a variety of different types of imposition patterns that can achieve this goal, depending on the way in which the sheet is folded.

Imprint
A list of books that form part of a publisher's overall output, usually identified by a particular style and logo. Large publishing companies may publish under a wide variety of imprints.

Indie publishing
Very small publishers (often publishing their own work – self-publishers) now able to use the technology of short-run, print-on-demand (POD) and e-book publishing to produce books independently from mainstream publishing.

IP: intellectual property
The concept of intellectual property lies at the basis of much commercial activity. Laws on intellectual property give owners of various intangible assets exclusive rights to exploit these assets. While IP covers a wide variety of property, including musical and artistic works, designs, trademarks, and inventions (through patent law), in publishing it is enforced through copyright law. In the digital culture, principles of IP and copyright have come under question in recent years and piracy, file-sharing, and illegal digital copying have been seen as threats to authors and publishers. The development of Open Access (OA) and Creative Commons (CC) are ways in which the producers and users of intellectual property have sought to address some of these issues.

IPR: intellectual property rights
The rights covered by IP.

ISBN: international standard book number
An ISBN is a unique number (formerly made up of ten digits and, since January 2007, 13 digits) that identifies a particular edition of a book.

ISO: international organization for standardization
The ISO (not IOS as the title of the organization would imply) is a non-governmental organization that develops and publishes international standards. Several of these standards are of particular relevance to publishers.

ISSN: international standard serial number
An eight-digit number that identifies a periodical publication in print or digital formats. A new standard, the ISSN-L, has been developed that will identify a group of the different media versions of a continuing resource, and there will now be only one ISSN-L regardless of how many different medium versions of a continuing resource exist.

Jobbers
Another name for wholesale distributors more commonly used in the US (particularly 'library jobbers').

JPEG: joint photographic experts group
A digital file format for images with complex pixel gradations. When JPEGs are compressed they lose some of the image quality so are not always suitable for use in publications.

lc: lower case
A standard abbreviation for lower case (small as opposed to capital letters) used in copy-editing and proofreading.

Loss leaders
A kind of sales promotion when a book is sold at a low price (often at or below cost) to encourage other more profitable sales. Both physical and online booksellers use loss-leader promotions to stimulate sales.

Manga
A type of comic that originated in Japan (representing about 40 per cent of the total book market), and now read and published around the world. Manga are read by people of all ages. Some contain violent and sexually explicit stories and images. They are often adapted to animated films and games, and are now available in e-book formats.

Mash-up
A work created by combining extracts from other works. Some authors have maintained that the mash-up provides an authentic transformation of the original content, and is therefore not an infringement of copyright.

Metadata
An extension of the sort of information about publications that can be found in a library catalogue (for example, ISBN). Metadata now includes a wide variety of information that identifies and describes a given publication. Digital technology both enables more metadata to be collected and disseminated, and it is seen as increasingly important in enabling potential readers of both p-books and e-books to discover and obtain publications.

Metrics
Quantitative data that is organized in a structured way and used to measure and compare market performance of different products, services and companies.

.mobi file
A domain name suffix used when mobile devices access the World Wide Web, including access to e-books.

Mobile app
An application that makes files that are readable on a mobile device.

m-book
An e-book that is formatted for reading on a smartphone or mobile device.

MS: manuscript
Originally the handwritten text produced by the author, the term continued to be used for works in typescript, and is still used even when texts are submitted to publishers in electronic form, either on disc or via email.

Net Book Agreement (NBA)
From 1900 until its eventual abolition in 1997, the Net Book Agreement in the UK and Ireland required booksellers to sell at a fixed retail price established by the publisher. Once the NBA was abolished, booksellers were able to compete on price and major bookstore chains, supermarkets and online booksellers were gradually able to command a greater share of the book market, and many independent booksellers went out of business.

Nielsen BookData
This information service provides publishing data services in more than 100 countries worldwide.

Nielsen BookScan
Collects retail sales information from point of sale systems in more than 31,500 bookshops around the world and uses this to provide market information to all parts of the book world.

NSR: net sales revenue (or receipts)
This is the money received by the publisher after any discounts or commissions have been given to customers. Royalties to authors are now usually paid on a percentage basis of the publisher's NSR, rather than on the list price of the book.

OA: open access
Open access is unrestricted online access to articles in journals, book chapters or other e-publications.

OCR: optical character recognition
The method of scanning physical images of text to produce machine-encoded text. It is widely used to convert books and documents into electronic files.

OP: out of print
When a publisher runs out of stock and decides not to reprint a book, it is declared out of print. Now that single copies of books can be printed using POD (see below) and many titles are available as e-books, far fewer books go OP than was the case in the past.

Opacity
The quality of paper that determines show-through. High opacity is needed to prevent show-through of images and solid print areas on the opposite side of the sheet.

Partwork
A publication on a particular subject, which is produced in regular instalments and is collectible. It does not normally carry advertising. It is sold mainly through subscription.

P-book: printed or physical book
This term is used to distinguish physical or printed books from the digital e-book.

PDF: portable data format
A file format used during the production process. Printers can use PDF files to process all the components of the book, including text and graphics, and produce a printing plate directly from the PDF file.

PE: printer's error
When marking up proofs of a new book, it is important to distinguish those errors that have been introduced during the production process. By marking a correction with 'PE' the proofreader is indicating that the error should be corrected at the printer's expense.

Pica
A unit traditionally used to measure type size, equivalent in size to the body of a 12-point em or 4.23 mm (approximately 1/6 of an inch). In order for pages of type to be readable, typesetters formerly agreed that a line of 12-point type should be between 17 and 33 pica in width, with similar limits suggested for smaller and larger type sizes.

Piracy
In publishing this is the unauthorized reproduction of copyright works.

Plagiarism
When an author deliberately copies someone else's work, using the same words and phrases, the work is said to be plagiarized. If such work is published, both the author and publisher may be liable to pay damages that result from the plagiarism.

PLR: public lending right
PLR provides payment to authors in respect of loans of their books made through libraries, and it has been particularly successful in providing middle-ranking authors with additional income. Starting in Denmark in 1946, PLR had spread to 29 countries by 2011. Following UK legislation in 1979, the first payments were made in 1984. The income authors receive from PLR is under threat from governments seeking to reduce expenditure and from the increased use of e-books.

POD: print (or publication) on demand
Using digital files to make single copies of books to be produced in response to individual orders.

POS: point of sale
Materials are used in bookshops and other retail environments to attract customers to new books, special offers, or other promotional offers. POS materials include posters, display units, and counter packs.

Product life cycle (PLC)
A marketing concept used to analyze the stages a new book goes through (launch, growth, maturity, saturation and decline). These stages are different for various types of book.

Promotion
Publishers and booksellers actively promote sales of books through paid print, TV and radio advertisements, catalogues and flyers, direct mail, posters, web advertising and a wide variety of other methods. In general, promotion entails an expense and is done according to an agreed budget, often in collaboration with other parts of the supply chain.

PSD: Photoshop document
Photoshop remains the dominant software that publishers use to create layered images. Basic Photoshop documents are saved with the suffix .psd.

Publicity
Publishers work with a wide variety of other companies to ensure that new books, authors, media tie-ins, TV and movies adaptations get publicity through other media channels. Publicity in the media or through personal appearances is important in creating a 'buzz' around the new publication, and in building brand awareness, viral marketing and word-of-mouth recommendations. It also reinforces cult authors and the celebrity status of media personalities.

Publisher's list
The list of books in a publisher's catalogue or seasonal offering that reflects the acquisition and commissioning policy of the firm and the market it is addressing with its publications.

Revenue
The income (receipts) that a business receives from its business activities. If a publishing company is to survive, its revenue must be sufficient to cover its costs.

RGB: red, green, blue
The primary colours; see entry for *CMYK*.

Rights
In publishing, rights refer to the ownership of, or permission to use a work for a specific purpose. The central right to publish a book (volume rights) is at the core of the author-publisher contract and there are numerous subsidiary rights such as translation rights.

RSS: really simple syndication
A way to publish frequently updated works, such as blog posts, or news, in a standardized format, which means that publishers can syndicate content automatically.

Running head
The text that appears at the top of the page of a printed book, used as an aid to navigating the printed work.

Samizdat
A type of clandestine self-publishing that originated in the Soviet Union in the twentieth century, now sometimes used to describe other sorts of dissident publishing.

Sans serif
A word that describes typefaces (like Univers and Ariel) in which the letters do not have 'ornaments'. San serif typefaces are commonly used for texts intended to be read on screen.

Self-publishing
When an author or organization publishes without a publisher.

SEO: search engine optimization
The practice of improving the ranking position of a website on Internet search engines. SEO seeks to increase the number of visitors to a website by such means as increasing hyperlinks, and adding key words. SEO is evaluated by monitoring the number and type of visitors to a website.

SGML: standard generalized markup language
SGML began in 1986 to provide a standard language in which documents could be shared between systems. It developed and formed the basis of HTML and XML.

Signature
A sheet of paper printed with four (or a multiple of four) pages, folded to form a section of a book. Most books are made up of a number of signatures that are folded and gathered to form what is known as a book block, which is then glued or sewn together, bound and trimmed to form the finished book.

Stet
Latin for 'let it stand', indicating that something that has been marked for correction should remain as it is. The action to remain unchanged is indicated by a row of dashes under the text.

Sticky content
Components of a website intended to motivate a user to return to that particular website or to spend longer periods of time on it. Can include features such as chat rooms, surveys and games.

STM: scientific, technical, medical
Scientific, technical and medical publishing encompasses a wide variety of books, journals and digital publications. STM publishing is one of the largest and most profitable sectors of publishing, and it operates on a global level with a small number of large companies dominating the market.

Territorial restrictions
Conditions imposed on publishers and/or booksellers that restrict the sale of a book in specified geographical markets. For example, a UK edition of a book may not be sold in the US and a US edition may not be sold in the UK market.

Tertiary
The third level of education that takes place in universities and colleges (after primary/elementary, secondary/high school levels of education).

TIFF: tagged image file format
A flexible way of storing halftone and colour bitmap images that gives better quality than a JPEG file.

Transmedia
The term used to describe e-publications that use a wide variety of media (video, audio).

Typo
A typographical error or misspelling. It is the job of the editor or proofreader to spot and correct typos before the publication goes into production.

uc: upper case
A standard abbreviation for upper case (capital letters) used in copy-editing and proofreading.

USP: unique selling proposition
When you are marketing any publication, you need to be clear what it is that makes it particularly useful and desirable to your target audience. Identifying the USP and communicating this to the people you think should be your customers is an essential component of marketing and promotion.

UX: user experience
The UX looks at positive or negative aspects of the way a user experiences a website. The quality of the UX will determine the user's attitude to the content, whether they will buy or recommend what is on offer, and determine whether the user will return to the website.

Vertical integration
When a company owns or controls different functions or processes in the entire publishing, printing and bookselling chain, such as a publisher owning a printer and/or bookseller, or an online retailer manufacturing and selling a device on which publishers' e-books can be read.

WIP: work in progress
A work in progress is a piece of work that is not yet finished. Most writers have at least one project like this, and some remain 'works in progress' for a long time, which can be very frustrating for their editors.

WIP: Women in Publishing
An association of women working in publishing in the UK. While a majority of the people working in publishing are women, there are far fewer women in senior management positions (in spite of a small number of female CEOs). There are similar organizations in several other countries.

XHTML: eXtensible HyperText Markup Language
It is a part of the XML markup languages that are extensions and versions of the widely-used Hypertext Markup Language (HTML), which is used to write web pages.

XML: extensible markup language
XML established a way of encoding documents in machine-readable form that is now at the basis of much of the software used by publishers in preparing text for publication.

Bibliography

Books about publishing

Ambrose, G and Harris, P (2010) *The Visual Dictionary of Pre-Press & Production.* Lausanne: AVA.

Anderson, C (2006) *The Long Tail: Why the Future of Business is Selling Less of More.* New York: Hyperion.

Bann, D (2011) *The All New Print Production Handbook.* London: RotoVision.

Baverstock, A, Carey, S and Bowen, S (2008) *How to Get a Job in Publishing: A Really Practical Guide to Careers in Books and Magazines.* London: A & C Black.

Baverstock, A (2008) *How to Market Books. 4th ed.* London: Kogan Page.

Bullock, A (2012) *Book Production: A Manual of Project and Production Management in Book Publishing.* London: Routledge.

Butcher, J (2006) *Butcher's Copy-editing: The Cambridge Handbook for Editors, Copy-editors and Proofreaders. 4th ed.* Cambridge: Cambridge University Press.

Clark, G, and Phillips, A (2008) *Inside Book Publishing. 4th ed.* London: Routledge.

Davis, G (2004) *Book Commissioning & Acquisition. 2nd ed.* London: Routledge.

Davis, G and Balkwill, R (2011) *The Professionals' Guide to Publishing.* London: Kogan Page.

Lanier, J (2010) *You Are Not a Gadget: A Manifesto.* London: Allen Lane.

Levine, R (2011) *Free Ride: How the Internet Is Destroying the Culture Business and How the Culture Business Can Fight Back.* London: Bodley Head.

Levine, M (2011) *The Fine Print of Self-Publishing. 4th ed.* Minneapolis: Bascom Hill.

Manguel, A (2008) *The City of Words.* New York & London: Continuum.

Owen, L (2010) *Clark's Publishing Agreements: A Book of Precedents, 8th Edition.* London: Bloomsbury.

Owen, L (2010) *Selling Rights. 6th ed.* London: Routledge.

Powers, A (2001) *Front Cover: Great Book Jackets and Cover Design.* London: Mitchell Beazley.

Richardson, P and Taylor, G (2008) *A Guide to the UK Publishing Industry.* London: The Publishers Association.

Thompson, J (2005) *Books in the Digital Age.* Cambridge: Polity.

Thompson, J (2010) *Merchants of Culture.* Cambridge: Polity.

University of Chicago Press (2010) *The Chicago Manual of Style: The Essential Guide for Writers, Editors and Publishers. 16th ed.* Chicago: University of Chicago Press.

Wischenbart, R (2011) *The Global 2011 eBook Market: Current Conditions & Future Projections.* Sebastopol (USA): O'Reilly Media.

Woll, T (2010) *Publishing for Profit: Successful Bottom-Line Management for Book Publishers. 4th ed.* Chicago: Chicago Review Press.

World Intellectual Property Organization (2008) *Managing Intellectual Property in the Book Publishing Industry.* Geneva: WIPO.

SHARP – The Society for the History of Authorship, Reading and Publishing – is a global network for book historians working in a broad range of scholarly disciplines. SHARP has more than 1,000 members in over 20 countries. Members conduct research on the composition, mediation, reception, survival, and transformation of written communication in material forms including marks on stone, script on parchment, printed books and periodicals, and new media. www.sharpweb.org

Book trade journals

Australia: Bookseller and Publisher
www.booksellerandpublisher.com.au
Canada: Quill and Quire
www.quillandquire.com
China: China Book International
www.cbi.gov.cn
Denmark: BogMarkedet
www.bogmarkedet.dk
France: Livres Hébdo
www.livreshebdo.fr
Germany: Buchreport
www.buchreport.de
India: Association of Publishers in India
www.publishers.org.in
Italy: Giornale della Librería
www.argentovivo.it
Netherlands: Boekblad
www.boekblad.nl
Norway: Bok Samfunn
www.bokogsamfunn.no
South Africa: Books Live
www.bookslive.co.za
Spain: Delibros
www.delibros.com
Sweden: Svensk Bokhandel
www.svb.se
United Kingdom: The Bookseller
www.thebookseller.com
United Kingdom: Printing News
www.myprintresource.com
United States: Publishers Weekly
www.publishersweekly.com
United States: American Printer
http://americanprinter.com

Internet newsletters

There are many book blogs and publishing websites that send out regular posts to subscribers. It can be easy to be overwhelmed. Here are some newsletters that you may like to subscribe to.

Europublishing
www.europublishing.info
Mediabistro
www.mediabistro.com/ebooknewser
Moco News
http://moconews.net
Paid Content
http://paidcontent.org and
http://paidcontent.co.uk
Publishing Perspectives
http://publishingperspectives.com
The Shatzkin Files
www.idealog.com

Some major prizes

The Man Booker Prize
www.themanbookerprize.com
Le Prix Goncourt
www.academie-goncourt.fr
International IMPAC Dublin Literary Award
www.impacdublinaward.ie
The Pulitzer Prize
www.pulitzer.org
Governor General's Literary Awards
www.canadacouncil.ca/prizes/ggla

Online resources

Thousands of publishers, publishers' associations and other organizations provide information on the Internet. Here are just a few.

National organizations

There are national publishing organizations in most countries, most of which can be found through the IPA. Here are a few of the biggest. (You should note that some information on the websites is password protected and only available to members of the association.)

Argentina: Cámara Argentina del Libro
www.editores.org.ar
Australia: Australian Publishers Association
www.publishers.asn.au
Brazil: Câmara Brasileira do Livro
www.cbl.org.br
China: General Administration of Press and Publication
www.gapp.gov.cn
France: Syndicat national de l'édition
www.sne.fr
Germany: Börsenverein des Deutschen Buchhandels
www.boersenverein.de
India: Association of Publishers in India
www.publishers.org.in
New Zealand: Publishers Association of New Zealand
www.bpanz.org.nz
United Kingdom: The Publishers Association
www.publishers.org.uk
United Kingdom: Independent Publishers Guild
www.ipg.uk.com
United Kingdom: The Society of Authors
www.societyofauthors.org
United States of America: Association of American Publishers
www.publishers.org
United States of America: National Association of College Stores
www.nacs.org

International organizations

Association of Learned and Professional Society Publishers (ALPSP)
www.alpsp.org
Berne Convention Website
www.wipo.int/treaties/en/ip/berne
Creative Commons
http://creativecommons.org
DOI (Digital Object Identifier)
www.doi.org
International Association of Scientific, Technical & Medical Publishers
www.stm-assoc.org
International Publishers Association
www.internationalpublishers.org
ISBN Association (International Standard Book Number)
www.isbn-international.org
ISSN International Centre (International Standard Serial Number)
www.issn.org
Nielsen SAN Agency (Standard Address Number)
www.san.nielsenbook.co.uk
PEN International
www.internationalpen.org.uk
World Intellectual Property Organization
www.wipo.int

The International Publishers Association (IPA) maintains a website that provides many useful links to international information on publishing.

Regional organizations

Africa: African Publishers Network (APNET)
www.african-publishers.net
Caribbean and Latin America: Centro Regional para el Fomento del Libro en América Latina y el Caribe (CERLALC)
www.cerlalc.org
South East Asia: ASEAN Book Publishers Association (ABPA)
www.abpa.asia

Sources of industry data

American Booksellers Alliance Indie Bound
www.bookweb.org/indiebound
American Booksellers Foundation for Free Expression
www.abffe.com
American Library Association
www.ala.org
Audio Publishers Association
www.audiopub.org
Book Industry Study Group
www.bisg.org
Department for Education School Curriculum (UK)
http://curriculum.qcda.gov.uk
Digital Book World
www.digitalbookworld.com
International Digital Publishing Forum
http://idpf.org
Nielsen BookData
www.nielsenbookdata.co.uk

Useful websites

AARP Magazine
www.aarp.org/magazine

Amazon
www.amazon.com

BBC/Horrible Histories
www.bbc.co.uk/cbbc/shows/horrible-histories

British Library
www.bl.uk

California Digital Library
www.cdlib.org

Cambridge Books Online
http://ebooks.cambridge.org

Cambridge University Press
www.cambridge.org

EBSCO
www.ebsco.com

Elle TV
www.elleuk.com/elleTV

e-scholarship programme at UC
www.escholarship.org

Faber and Faber Independent Alliance
www.faber.co.uk/about/independent-alliance

The Feminist Press
www.feministpress.org

For Dummies
www.dummies.com

Fortune Magazine
www.fortune.magazine.co.uk

Grove Music Online
www.oxfordmusiconline.com

Grove Art Online
www.oxfordartonline.com

The Guardian
www.guardian.co.uk

Horrible Histories
www.horrible-histories.co.uk

Huffington Post
www.huffingtonpost.com

The Independent
www.independent.co.uk

MIT Open Courseware
http://ocw.mit.edu/courses

The MIT Press
http://mitpress.mit.edu

Oxford Dictionary of National Biography
www.oxforddnb.com

Oxford English Dictionary
www.oed.com

Oxford University Press
http://global.oup.com

Persephone Books
www.persephonebooks.co.uk

Project Gutenberg
www.gutenberg.org

Saga Magazine
www.saga.co.uk/saga-magazine.aspx

TED
www.ted.com

UC Publishing Services
www.ucpress.edu/partners.php

University of California Press
www.ucpress.edu

University Press Scholarship Online
www.universitypressscholarship.com

Virago Books
www.viragobooks.net

The Waste Land
http://touchpress.com/titles/thewasteland

The Women's Press
www.the-womens-press.com

The publishing year: book fairs and other major publishing events

During the year there are many established events in the publishing calendar. Some of these have grown from book publishing events to encompass all aspects of digital publishing. In addition to these publishing events, there are many conventions, conferences and seminars that attract librarians, booksellers, publishing software designers, printers, designers and just about everyone who is involved with the publishing business.

Here are just some of the important events that an agent, publisher or firm involved in book distribution might attend in a given year. In spite of all the possibilities for electronic communication (phone, e-mail, instant messaging, conference calls, and video-messaging, skyping, podcasting and live streaming), publishers still like to meet up to discuss business with their colleagues face-to-face.

Month	Event
January	Digital Book World (New York, USA) <www.digitalbookworld.com> Festival Internationale de la Bande Dessinée (Angoulême, France) <www.bdangouleme.com>
March	Abu Dhabi International Book Fair (Abu Dhabi) <www.adbookfair.com> Salon du livre (Paris, France) <www.salondulivreparis.com> Bologna Children's Book Fair (Bologna, Italy) <www.bookfair.bolognafiere.it>
April	The London Book Fair (London, UK) <www.londonbookfair.co.uk>
June	BookExpo America (New York, USA) <www.bookexpoamerica.com> Special Library Association Annual Conference (various cities, USA) <www.sla.org> American Library Association Annual Conference (various cities, USA) <www.alaannual.org>
July	Tokyo International Book Fair (Tokyo, Japan) <www.bookfair.jp> Hong Kong Book Fair (Hong Kong, China) <www.hkbookfair.com>
August	Beijing International Book Fair (Beijing, China) <www.bibf.net>
September	Göteborg International Book Fair (Göteborg, Sweden) <www.bok-bibliotek.se>
October	Frankfurt Book Fair (Frankfurt, Germany) <www.frankfurt-book-fair.com>
November	Guadalajara International Book Fair (Guadalajara, Mexico) <www.fil.com.mx>

'The Gutenberg era is not about to come to an end. Printed books will still exist. After television, we still have cinemas and radio. There is no need to fear that bound books will only be found in museums, connoisseur's collections, and in antique markets, or considered curiosities the same way we now view eight-track tapes. The book industry that we know and understand today will continue to thrive, but it will be transformed by e-books and e-readers.'

PWC Report, 'Turning the Page: The Future of eBooks', 2010

Index

Page numbers in *italics* denote illustrations.

Picture credits and acknowledgements

p. 18 The Art Archive/Bibliothèque Municipale de Toulouse/Kharbine-Tapabor/Coll. J. Vigne; p. 19 The Art Archive/ Superstock; The Art Archive/British Library; p. 20 Wilhei/Wikimedia Commons; p. 21 © Bettmann/Corbis; p. 22/3 courtesy Penguin Group UK; p. 24 courtesy the Tourism Entity, Government of Buenos Aires City; p. 27 courtesy Amazon.com, Inc.; p. 32 Reed Exhibitions Ltd; p. 35 courtesy Wordsworth Editions; p. 43 courtesy Bloomsbury Publishing; p. 44 *The Lost Symbol* by Dan Brown courtesy Random House, Inc.; p. 45 cover from *The Little Prince* by Antoine de Saint Exupéry (San Diego: Harcourt, 1943) courtesy Houghton Mifflin Harcourt; p. 45 *Dreams From My Father* by Barack Obama courtesy Canongate Books; p. 46 *The Saga of Darren Shan Volume 5*, © 2010 Darren Shan and © 2010 Takahiro Arai, HarperCollins Publishers Ltd; p. 49 cover of *ACTA Oecologica Information Journal of Ecology*, volume 35, No. 6, November-December 2009 © Elsevier; p. 49 © 2011 *The American Journal of Investigative Pathology*; p. 51 courtesy Guinness World Records™; p. 53 courtesy Amazon. com, Inc.; p. 55 MichaelJay/iStockphoto LP; p. 57 *Saga Magazine*; p. 59 *The Bookseller*; p. 64 courtesy Amazon.com, Inc.; p. 71 *The Cat in the Hat Comes Back* by Dr. Seuss © 1958, 1986 by Dr. Seuss Enterprises L. P., HarperCollins Publishers Ltd; p. 72 *Axolotl Roadkill* courtesy Ullstein Buchverlage GmbH; p. 72 Creative Commons; p. 73 Jane Bown, courtesy Faber and Faber; p. 77 *The Wonders of the Solar System* © 2010 Professor Brian Cox, HarperCollins Publishers Ltd; p. 79 Hong Kong Trade Development Council – Hong Kong Book Fair 2010; p. 79 Jacqueline Wilson website courtesy Random House Children's Publishers; p. 80 © Reuters/Corbis; p. 83 *Torn* courtesy Amanda Hocking/Hocking Books; p. 85 courtesy Kirkus Media LCC; p. 86 Alex Heimann; p. 87 Peter Hirth/Frankfurter Buchmesse; p. 95 Foyles; p. 97 *Cabal* by Michael Dibdin courtesy Faber and Faber; p. 98 Julie Powell courtesy Little, Brown Book Group; p. 113 *Microsoft Windows 7 & Office 2010 For Dummies* by Andy Rathbone and Wallace Wang, © 2010 Wiley Publishing, Inc., reprinted with permission of John Wiley & Sons, Inc.; p. 119 Art Meets Matter; p. 127 Dudarev Mikhail/Shutterstock.com, Vagabond/Shutterstock.com, Marcus Gann/ Shutterstock.com, Christos Georghiou/Shutterstock.com; p. 128 *An Intimate Life of Paul McCartney* © 2010 Howard Sounes, HarperCollins Publishers Ltd; p. 131 Iakov Filimonov/Shutterstock.com; p. 130 courtesy Xerox Corporation; p. 137 Michele Perbillini/Shutterstock.com; p. 139 *Horrible Histories: Terrible Tudors*, text copyright © Terry Deary and Neil Tonge, 1993, 1999, illustration © Martin Brown, 1993, 1999 reproduced with the permission of Scholastic Ltd; p. 144 Alex Heimann; p. 146 *The Waste Land* app courtesy Touchpress.com; p. 149 *Mastering the Art of French Cooking* by Julia Child, courtesy Random House, Inc.; p. 150 *Indignez-Vous!* Stéphane Hessel courtesy Indigène éditions; p. 151 courtesy Kobobooks.com; p. 157 courtesy Amazon.com, Inc.; p. 158 Bash Street Kids © *The Beano*, DC Thomson & Co. Ltd; p. 159 courtesy The American Book Center, Amsterdam; p. 161 courtesy Cambridge University Press; p. 166 *They Do It With Mirrors* by Agatha Christie © 1952 Agatha Christie Ltd (a Chorion company), HarperCollins Publishers Ltd; p. 168 Heathcliff O'Malley/Rex Features; p. 169 courtesy Daunt Books; p. 171 John Locke; p. 173 London News Pictures/Rex Features; p. 174 EON/Danjaq/Kobal; p. 175 arindambanerjee/Shutterstock.com; p. 176 Syngrafi Corp.; p. 177 *Bad Luck and Trouble* by Lee Child, courtesy Random House, Inc.; p. 184 courtesy Persephone Books; p. 185 *The Enchanted April* by Elizabeth von Arnim, Virago Press an imprint of Little, Brown Book Group.

All reasonable attempts have been made to trace, clear and credit the copyright holders of the images reproduced in this book. However, if any credits have been inadvertently omitted, the publisher will endeavour to incorporate amendments in future editions.

Acknowledgements

Over several decades I have been fortunate to know many inspirational and idiosyncratic publishing people from all over the world. Much of what I think about books and the way they are created, made and marketed arises from time spent with these colleagues, too numerous to name, and I am grateful for having had the chance to learn from all of them. I am equally grateful to all the students from so many different countries, whose enthusiasm and commitment to the future of publishing reinforces my conviction that there is something particularly worthwhile about working with books.

Writing a book about publishing in a time of great change in the book world is a risky business, and I am grateful to Georgia Kennedy at AVA for persuading me that such a task was both possible and necessary, and to my editor, Kate Duffy, for her professional support and friendly encouragement as the project developed into the book you hold in your hands.

The publishers would like to thank David Emblidge, Dr Sally Hughes, Dr James Dearnley, Nick Canty and Brenda Stones.